Where in the World

Is Roxton, Texas?

Words of Wisdom from a
Small Town Pastor

Louis A. Holmes

MaxHolt
Media

(<u>NOTE</u>: Every individual *WORD OF WISDOM* page ends with a note-taking space. If you are reading this in the Kindle format you may need to acquire a paper notepad, unless your e-Reader has note-taking capability.)

Cover design by Max Holt Media
Cover art byDreamstime.com

ISBN: 13: 978-1-944537-08-1

Published by: Max Holt Media
303 Cascabel Place,
Mount Juliet, TN 37122
www.maxholtmedia.com
On facebook at www.facebook.com/maxholtmedia
    Email – max@maxholtmedia.com
    Twitter - @maxholtmedia

INTRODUCTION

It was in the fall of 1962 that my parents, Louis E. and Edna Holmes, went into full time service for the Lord in Grapevine, Texas. Bethel Baptist Church was, at the time, a country church in a small town. Things were pretty slow at first, then accelerated to a faster pace over the 1960's. As the church grew provision had to be made to meet the needs of the people. Bethel Baptist Church went through four building programs during those years. In all of it, the people, the town, the church, and the family made many precious memories for me in that place. Little did I know that years later spiritual application could be made with these instances in my life.

Today, Roxton, Texas reminds me of Grapevine, Texas in 1962. I serve as the bi-vocational pastor of First Baptist Church in Roxton, Texas. Life is simpler and everyone knows everybody. The café in town opens at 6:30 am on weekdays and at 6:31 many folks will already be there eating breakfast with thick conversation about everything imaginable. We have a bank, a Post Office, and the one gas station is still full service.

Researchers say that there are approximately 150 million Americans who live in small towns. Small towns are unique because they are places where families are still important, kids still say the PLEDGE in school, teams still pray at football games, veterans are still honored in the town square and churches still preach the *gospel truth*.

The City of Roxton has a nick-name: The "Biggest Little City in Texas." If one of our own needs help, we help him. A fundraiser for someone is always a success with the citizens giving liberally to the cause.

The purpose of this book is to highlight life in a small church and a small town and pass along some encouraging words from a Biblical perspective.

DEDICATION

I would like to dedicate this book to my parents for their faithfulness in following the leading of the LORD. Without their obedience to Him, I would have never had the opportunity to experience life as a preacher's kid. While at times life could be difficult in the parsonage, my life was enriched with personal experiences that would take a lifetime to express on paper.

A big thank-you to my lovely wife, Jan. Thank you for loving me and staying by my side. It has been a great adventure.

Thank you to the people of First Baptist Church in Roxton, Texas. It is certainly a pleasure to be your Pastor, and to labor together with you for the LORD.

I would also like to acknowledge the people of Bethel Baptist Church in Grapevine, Texas, for their faithfulness to the LORD. The church has been a lighthouse for the Word of God. Continue on in these last days.

Thank you to the people of Roxton, Texas, for making Roxton the "biggest little city" in Texas.

And thank you to Kris Rutherford and the Roxton Progress for publishing my articles. Perhaps together we were able to make a difference in the life of someone needing encouragement. And finally, thank you to Kris Rutherford for recommending that I compile these articles in the first place.

CONTENTS

1

New Year – New Beginning

Living in the small town of Grapevine, Texas in the early 1960's we would get together as a church on New Year's Eve to end the old year and begin the New Year right. We called it a *Watch Night Service*. The ladies would bring various foods for our mid-service break. The young boys would do a survey of the foods with discussion as to the author of that dish.

The service would begin promptly at 7:30 pm with some old fashioned hymns and lots of prayer. We all settled in for the four and a half hours ahead until midnight. Various men of the church would give us simple devotions and we would sing some more. Around 9:30 pm we would have our break. Then about 10:15 pm we would gather again for the remainder of the service. Finally, Dad would preach a charge to us and then we would all gather at the altar to pray in the New Year at midnight.

And then there was the matter of New Year's resolutions. We asked each other "What is your New Year's resolution?"

I have heard that the definition of insanity is "to do the same thing over and over expecting different results." Many of us will sometimes live in that rut of insanity. Of course we know what the definition of a rut is…A grave with both ends knocked out!

One thing about the New Year is that the only issues we have in the beginning of the New Year are those issues we carry over from the old year. The New Year is fresh and new and we view this as an opportunity to make things better. Many people will make New Year's resolutions, taking the opportunity to set things right. Unfortunately, most resolutions are doomed to failure after a short while. Some of the top resolutions are to lose weight, quit smoking, save more and spend less, among others. So here we are, having fallen into the yearly ritual of desiring change but not sticking with it. We end up doing the same thing over and over expecting different results. Sounds like insanity.

I will probably push a lot of you out of your comfort zone, but here is a short list of New Year's resolutions you might consider:
1.   Go to church every Sunday.
2.   Build a relationship with God.
3.   Spend time reading the Bible.
4.   Spend time in prayer.
5.   Use your gifts and talents to help someone else.
6.   Spend less time on the internet and gaming.
7.   Turn the television OFF!

God desires that we live our life abundantly. In the book of John chapter 10 verse 10 it says,

"The thief cometh not, but for to steal, and to kill, and to destroy: I am come that they might have life, and that they might have it more abundantly."

Jesus compares our lives in the hand of a thief to our lives being in His care. I believe the devil is a thief with an agenda to keep us trodden down in this life. Jesus, on the other hand, desires the best for us.

I am asking you to consider giving God a try. You might be uneasy about the idea of a church service, hearing a sermon, and spending time reading the Bible. But, I hope you will look for a church like ours. At First Baptist Church in Roxton I do all I can to make people's experiences in church pleasant. I have one purpose, and that is to bring everyone closer to God. I do that by teaching about who God is, what He has done, and how He relates to us. The LORD God is great! He is loving, He is truth, He is goodness, He is kindness, He is wise, and He is merciful. He desires the best for you...an abundant life filled with love and peace. One thing I know for sure...when the going gets tough it is good to know He is there.

Additional Scriptures

"So he fed them according to the integrity of his heart; and guided them by the skilfulness of his hands."
Psalm 78:72

"And they sang together by course in praising and giving thanks unto the LORD; because he is good, for his mercy endureth for ever toward Israel. And all the people shouted with a great shout, when they praised the LORD, because the foundation of the house of the LORD was laid."
Ezra 3:11

"For the LORD is good; his mercy is everlasting; and his truth endureth to all generations."
Psalm 100:5

"Come unto me, all ye that labour and are heavy laden, and I will give you rest."
Matthew 11:28

"Blessed is the man that walketh not in the counsel of the ungodly, nor standeth in the way of sinners, nor sitteth in the seat of the scornful. 2 But his delight is in the law of the LORD; and in his law doth he meditate day and night. 3 And he shall be like a tree planted by the rivers of water, that bringeth forth his fruit in his season; his leaf also shall not wither; and whatsoever he doeth shall prosper."
Psalm 1:1-3

"Let your conversation be without covetousness; and be content with such things as ye have: for he hath said, I will never leave thee, nor forsake thee."
Hebrews 13:5

Notes:

2

The Joy of Bubbly Milk

I have a friend, Lorene, whose son, Steve, works as an interim pastor. He helps churches that are looking for a pastor, by giving them the Word of God and removing the pressures of immediately finding a pastoral candidate. Steve will stay as long as necessary, but tries to limit his stay to about a year. Lorene mentioned to me that Steve was Interim Pastor at First Baptist Church in Roxton and to pray for him. Roxton stuck in my mind.

After a week or two I asked Lorene again about the church in Roxton. She said they had reviewed a couple of candidates, but were still searching. I had just resigned a church and felt like a fish out of water since I had no place to serve. I met Steve in a Braum's Ice Cream Store parking lot to give him my resume.

In the meantime, I went on a *Prayer Drive* to Roxton, Texas. Is it possible that God would want me to serve Him in Roxton? One does not go to Roxton by accident, you have to go there on purpose. I drove by the church and saw the stately facilities. Then I went to the downtown drag, and saw the bank and the store. Driving through the neighborhoods I saw a lot of people hurting that needed the Lord. My heart was moved to share with them the *Bubbly Milk* of knowing the LORD God. The following is how I learned of *Bubbly Milk*.

You never know when you will learn something extraordinary. I have learned to keep a vigilant watch, ever ready to embrace new ideas from reliable sources.

Living in a preacher's home I met a lot of people. Missionaries were the most common visitors to our humble parsonage. I met people that devoted their life to spreading the Gospel of Jesus Christ to people of foreign countries...Japan, India, Mexico, Australia, Guatemala, Brazil, and more. Some of these people were quite unique, but all were a privilege to know.

One time we had the privilege of hosting a young couple in our home that was raising support so they could go to New Guinea as missionaries. They were raised in the hills of Tennessee, bringing with them all the charm of their upbringing.

Our home was open to the missionaries. Anything they wanted they could have.

I remember one day when Gloria went to the refrigerator to get a glass of milk. I watched as Gloria took the milk jug and shook it vigorously for a couple of seconds before pouring her milk. Curious, I asked why she shook the milk first. Gloria said she liked the *bubbly* in her milk! I was intrigued by what I had learned and thought I should give that a try because all the bubbles I had had in my milk were then I blew them in with a straw.

A few minutes later I inconspicuously went to the kitchen, took the jug of milk out of the refrigerator, shook it vigorously for a couple of seconds, and poured me a glass of *bubbly milk*. It was really good! To this day I shake the jug before pouring another bubbly glass. It's really special if you have chocolate milk!

The Bible says in Psalm chapter 34 and verse 8:

"Taste and see that the LORD is good."

The verse also says that people are blessed when they trust in God. I hope you are one of those who trust in God. God is so good. Perhaps it's time to come to church again to rediscover the bubbly joy that God can bring to your life.

Additional Scriptures

"Surely goodness and mercy shall follow me all the days of my life: and I will dwell in the house of the LORD forever."
Psalm 23:6

"The eyes of the LORD are in every place, beholding the evil and the good."
Proverbs 15:3

"Then said Hezekiah to Isaiah, Good is the word of the LORD which thou hast spoken. He said moreover, For there shall be peace and truth in my days."
Isaiah 39:8

"Afterward shall the children of Israel return, and seek the LORD their God, and David their king; and shall fear the LORD and his goodness in the latter days."
Hosea 3:5

"Knowing that whatsoever good thing any man doeth, the same shall he receive of the Lord, whether he be bond or free."
Ephesians 6:8

"And when all the children of Israel saw how the fire came down, and the glory of the LORD upon the house, they bowed themselves with their faces to the ground upon the pavement, and worshipped, and praised the LORD, saying, For he is good; for his mercy endureth for ever."
II Chronicles 7:3

Notes

The New Preacher

Here in Roxton, Texas we have four churches. There is the Methodist Church, the predominately black congregations of Baptist and Holiness, and then there is First Baptist Church in Roxton. As a rule, the churches cooperate with each other on special events. From the very beginning I wanted the people of First Baptist Church and the citizens of Roxton to know that the new preacher is always up for a good laugh.

There is a joke I heard many years about a new preacher that came to town. The two old preachers in town wanted to extend their friendship by inviting the new preacher to go fishing.

It wasn't long that all three preachers were in the boat fishing not too far from the shore. Just up the hill from the shore was a convenience store.

A few minutes after they arrived to their favorite fishing spot the first old preacher said, "I need some more bait...I'll be right back." Then the first old preacher got out of the boat, walked across the water, went to the store, and came back to the boat. The new preacher was impressed.

A few minutes later the second old preacher spoke up, "I need some more fishing line...I'll be right back." Then the second old preacher got out of the boat, walked across the water, went to the store, and came back to the boat. The new preacher was very impressed now.

Feeling the pressure to be an equal to the two old preachers, the new preacher had to think of a reason to go to the store. He also figured the walking on the water would be an affirmation of his faith. Finally an idea came to him. "I forgot my fishing hooks," he said. "I'm going to the store and I'll be right back." The new preacher got out of the boat, took three steps on the water and then with a great fall went right under the waves...SPLASH!

The first old preacher leaned over to the second old preacher and said, "Reckon we should tell him about that row of stumps?"

It is a privilege for me to serve as the pastor of First Baptist Church in Roxton. However, I'm not perfect; I can't walk on water. Only the Lord Jesus could do that. Furthermore, I don't know where the stumps are, if you know what I mean. I can only promise to do the best I can as a minister of the Gospel; the Good News of Jesus Christ.

I hope that someday soon you will find your way to Roxton, Texas and come to First Baptist Church to worship with us, and meet a preacher that can't walk on water!

Additional Scriptures

"But we preach Christ crucified, unto the Jews a stumbling block, and unto the Greeks foolishness;"
I Corinthians 1:23

"Preach the word; be instant in season, out of season; reprove, rebuke, exhort with all long suffering and doctrine."
II Timothy 4:2

"I have preached righteousness in the great congregation: lo, I have not refrained my lips, O LORD, thou knowest."
Psalm 40:9

"The Spirit of the LORD God is upon me; because the LORD hath anointed me to preach good tidings unto the meek; he hath sent me to bind up the brokenhearted, to proclaim liberty to the captives, and the opening of the prison to them that are bound;"
Isaiah 61:1

"9 For though I be free from all men, yet have I made myself servant unto all, that I might gain the more. 20 And unto the Jews I became as a Jew, that I might gain the Jews; to them that are under the law, as under the law, that I might gain them that are under the law; 21 To them that are without law, as without law, (being not without law to God, but under the law to Christ,) that I might gain them that are without law. 22 To the weak became I as weak, that I might gain the weak: I am made all things to all men, that I might by all means save some. 23 And this I do for the gospel's sake, that I might be partaker thereof with you."

I Corinthians 9:19-23

*"And he said unto them, Go ye into all the world,
and preach the gospel to every creature."
Mark 16:15*

Notes:

4

The Emptiness of Instant Gratification

When I was around eight years old and school was out for the summer I would go to Aunt Neecie's, my Mom's older sister, to spend a week with my cousin Robert. Back then I called him Bob. It was great fun to be there. We would fly model rockets, ride bicycles, catch horny toad lizards, and race slot cars. For me it was an escape from the rigors of being a preacher's kid and life in the parsonage.

One time Aunt Neecie had to go to town and took me and Bob along. Back in those days we did not have any money, but Aunt Neecie dug around in her big purse and found a dime to give each of us boys. We were overjoyed...John D. Rockefeller never had it so good. We were going to the drug store for an old fashioned fountain treat!

When we arrived at the drug store there was one of those rocking horses on the sidewalk in front that was calling to me. I really wanted the treat, but I wanted to ride the horse too. The cost to ride the horse was ten cents. One silver dime. I mulled around the horse as it called my name. I walked up to the horse and touched his nose. It wasn't long I was sitting in the saddle.

Bob was talking about going inside the store to the fountain for a treat, but I was on the horse. I knew that once I inserted the dime into the coin slot of the horse my ride would commence. With a gentle release I heard the clink of the coin navigating its way to the coin box...a moment later I was punching cows and chasing Indians from the wagon train. A matter of seconds later, the ride was over.

Inside the drug store my cousin Bob ordered a treat for ten cents. I watched with envy as he sat there on the stool in front of the counter and enjoyed his treat. *"It's not fair,"* I thought, *"He has a treat and I don't."* It was a teachable moment. Aunt Neecie gently reminded me that I had spent my ten cents on the horse and Bob saved his ten cents for the treat.

The Bible says in Psalm chapter 90 and verse 12,

"So teach us to number our days, that we may apply our hearts unto wisdom."

I have witnessed in my years where people have spent all they have of their life just to ride the horse, while ignoring the good things that God has in store for their lives.

The Bible also says in James, Chapter 4 verse 14, that life is very short.

"For what is your life? It is even a vapor that appears for a little time, and then vanishes away."

If you check the obituaries you will find the final memorial for those people whose life has vanished away. One day, your final memorial will be there too.

Instead of spending your life on the emptiness of instant gratification of the things in this world, look to God to see what He has in store for you. God desires the best for you.

Additional Scriptures

"But none of these things move me, neither count I my life dear unto myself, so that I might finish my course with joy, and the ministry, which I have received of the Lord Jesus, to testify the gospel of the grace of God."
Acts 20:24

"Ye have sown much, and bring in little; ye eat, but ye have not enough; ye drink, but ye are not filled with drink; ye clothe you, but there is none warm; and he that earneth wages earneth wages to put it into a bag with holes."
Haggai 1:6

"Now therefore thus saith the LORD of hosts; Consider your ways."
Haggai 1:5

"O satisfy us early with thy mercy; that we may rejoice and be glad all our days."
Psalm 90:14

"The righteous eateth to the satisfying of his soul: but the belly of the wicked shall want."
Proverbs 13:25

"For all that is in the world, the lust of the flesh, and the lust of the eyes, and the pride of life, is not of the Father, but is of the world."
I John 2:16

Notes:

Lessons from My First Boss

There was a gracious man in my dad's church named Melvin McCrary. He was faithful to God and the church, and was very polite and kind. A time or two the McCrary's invited our family over for a meal and Bro. Mac, as we called him, could make some BBQ chicken that was absolutely wonderful. As I am writing this I can almost taste his chicken...it was that good.

Bro. Mac had started a janitorial service being noted for the quality work he did. However, it became a challenge sometimes because it was difficult to get his employees to commit to the odd hours required in janitorial work.

One day on his way to a job he came by the church. I was fifteen years old and trying to mind my own business. Bro. Mac went into Dad's office for a chat. The next thing I know Dad came out with Bro. Mac and told me to help him for the day. I obediently got into the van and saw the mop and bucket, the dust mops, and the buffing machines. Bro. Mac started the van and off we went. It appeared that I was hired.

It wasn't long until Bro. Mac began taking me on some evening jobs cleaning offices. One night I was cleaning around a break area and I bumped one of those glass coffee decanters. Yep, you guessed right...it broke. I felt embarrassed and scared I would get into trouble. There were several decanters so I figured they would never miss one. I slipped the broken decanter into the trash and promptly carried it out. No one would ever know...so I thought.

A couple of days later we went out again to clean offices. Bro. Mac took me off to the side to talk to me about the broken coffee decanter. It was missed and the customer called inquiring about it. He said that in this line of work something like a broken coffee decanter will happen every once in a while and it is OK to say something. He said it is better to let him know so he can replace the decanter rather than letting the customer discover it and reporting a complaint. I learned a valuable life lesson that night. It was OK to admit I'm not perfect.

It is safe to say that none of us are perfect. We are all human and we all make plenty of mistakes. Always remember that God is an awesome God that relates Himself to us with all that He is. The best thing anyone can do is to admit their mistakes to God, ask for forgiveness, and then forsake the mistake so it won't happen again. God is faithful. He is always loving and compassionate. God is always willing to forgive. And God truly cares for us even when we make mistakes. He knows we are not perfect yet He loves us anyway.

The last few years I have studied more about what God is like and how He desires to relate to us. I would like to pass that information on to you, but a 500 word theme twice a month in the paper would take a long time.

"And there are also many other things which Jesus did, the which, if they should be written every one, I suppose that even the world itself could not contain the books that should be written."
John 21:25

Additional Scriptures

"Let the wicked forsake his way, and the unrighteous man his thoughts: and let him return unto the LORD, and he will have mercy upon him; and to our God, for he will abundantly pardon."
Isaiah 55:7

"But there is forgiveness with thee, that thou mayest be feared."
Psalm 130:4

"Blessed is the man unto whom the LORD imputeth not iniquity, and in whose spirit there is no guile."
Psalm 32:2

"Blessed is the man to whom the Lord will not impute sin."
Romans 4:8

"And be found in him, not having mine own righteousness, which is of the law, but that which is through the faith of Christ, the righteousness which is of God by faith:"
Philippians 3:9

"Wherefore, beloved, seeing that ye look for such things, be diligent that ye may be found of him in peace, without spot, and blameless."
II Peter 3:14

Notes:

Lessons from My First Boss – Part Two

I mentioned to you that Melvin McCrary was my first boss. He was kind, humorous, and had gifted insight to the ways of life. He owned a janitorial service and hired me to work for him part time.

After a short time of working for Bro. Mac, as he liked to be called, he advanced me from a dust mop to the wet mop. I took it as a promotion. I count the hours at the ignorant end of a wet mop directing the business end as golden; building maturity and character.

We were cleaning the floors in a grocery store, going aisle by aisle with a scrubbing machine and I following behind with a wet mop to rinse. Bro. Mac came by to check on my progress. I was really proud thinking that I had begun to master my craft. We had scrubbed about half of the store and my mop water was really getting dirty.

"Louis," he said, "your mop water is getting dirty."

"Yes sir," I replied proudly, "I'm getting a lot of dirt off the floor."

With his gentle manner he disagreed with me, "You're putting down more dirt with that dirty rinse water than what you are picking up." Then came the words of wisdom, "Your floor is only as clean as your rinse water. Change your rinse water often."

That was an *"Ah-Ha"* moment. Similarly, your life is only as clean as your mind and your heart.

"For as he thinketh in his heart, so is he:"
Proverbs 23:7a

If you could pour all the thoughts out of your head into a mop bucket would they be dirty enough they need to be changed? (I know, that's a scary thought.)

It was the Apostle Paul that gave us direction on how to think.

"Finally, brethren, whatsoever things are true, whatsoever things are honest, whatsoever things are just, whatsoever things are pure, whatsoever things are lovely, whatsoever things are of good report; if there be any virtue, and if there be any praise, think on these things."
Philippians 4:8

These profound words can be used to test the things you bring into your life. Does the television program you watch measure up to this test? How about the movie you want to see. How about that magazine, or even your conversation with another person. Does it measure up as true, honest, just, pure, and lovely?

Spending time with God by reading the Bible and prayer will really help clean your mind. Jesus spoke these wonderful words:

"Now ye are clean through the word which I have spoken unto you."
John 15:3

And sound words of wisdom from the psalmist:

"How shall a young man cleanse his way? By taking heed thereto according to the Word of God."
Psalm 119:9

After listening to Bro. Mac about my rinse water I immediately went and poured out that dirty water. I then filled the mop bucket with fresh water and returned to my duties. I changed my rinse water frequently after that, knowing now that my floor was really clean. I hope yours is too.

Additional Scriptures

"Then will I sprinkle clean water upon you, and ye shall be clean: from all your filthiness, and from all your idols, will I cleanse you."
Ezekiel 36:25

"Husbands, love your wives, even as Christ also loved the church, and gave himself for it; 26 That he might sanctify and cleanse it with the washing of water by the word, 27 That he might present it to himself a glorious church, not having spot, or

wrinkle, or any such thing; but that it should be holy and without blemish."
Ephesians 5:25-27

"Wash you, make you clean; put away the evil of your doings from before mine eyes; cease to do evil;"
Isaiah 1:16

"If we confess our sins, he is faithful and just to forgive us our sins, and to cleanse us from all unrighteousness."
I John 1:9

"Create in me a clean heart, O God; and renew a right spirit within me."
Psalm 51:10

"Now ye are clean through the word which I have spoken unto you."
John 15:3

Notes:

When Dreams Don't Come True

Sometimes I think the world system has done a disservice by telling people that all their dreams will come true. I have had dreams of doing something or becoming something other than I am and I'm sure most of you have too. The reality is that we usually dream of more than what we are willing to work at becoming.

I have always admired doctors because it takes an extraordinary amount of work and determination to accomplish that dream. It takes a lot of school, college, post graduate work, internship, and residency before they can hang out their shingle and practice medicine. The truth is, neither you nor I would want to place our health in the hands of anyone with less.

If you were to run a survey you would find that most folks have pretty much the same dream; getting a great paying job, to own a home, to drive an exotic car, or becoming rich. One common denominator to these dreams and desires is money. Many people have exhausted themselves in this pursuit of gaining money and usually have little to show for it. Without the money there are no riches, no hot car, no big house, and so on. People who are obsessed with these things but never gain them are never happy. The joy of their life is based on what they have or don't have in the way of material possessions.

The Apostle Paul summed it up in his letter to the church at Philippi;

"Not that I speak in respect of want: for I have learned, in whatsoever state I am, therewith to be content. I know both how to be abased, and I know how to abound: every where and in all things I am instructed both to be full and to be hungry, both to abound and to suffer need."
Philippians 4:11-12

Wow, what great words! The Apostle Paul was a man that could have been incredibly wealthy, but he chose to follow Jesus Christ and learned the joy that comes from Jesus the Son of God. As a result, the Apostle Paul was not consumed with dreams of earthly things, but on the worth of the knowledge of Jesus Christ.

If you have a dream for great wealth, a new car, or a new home, then hang in there and work for it. Who knows, it is not out of the realm of possibility. But until your dreams come true and even after your dream comes true, remember to cherish the things in your life that you already have that are greater than the dream of material things. Thank God for your extended family. Thank God for your spouse and your children. Thank God for your health; it's a precious gift. Thank God for a country where we live in peace.

Like many of you I too have had dreams that did not come true. Now that I am a little older and hopefully wiser, I can see where most of these dreams and desires held little intrinsic value. You have only one life to live, don't dream it away. Hold fast to the blessings that you already have. You will be glad you did.

Additional Scriptures

"Lay not up for yourselves treasures upon earth, where moth and rust doth corrupt, and where thieves break through and steal: 20 But lay up for yourselves treasures in heaven, where neither moth nor rust doth corrupt, and where thieves do not break through nor steal: 21 For where your treasure is, there will your heart be also."
Matthew 6:19-21

"Sell that ye have, and give alms; provide yourselves bags which wax not old, a treasure in the heavens that faileth not, where no thief approacheth, neither moth corrupteth."
Luke 12:33

"For where your treasure is, there will your heart be also."
Luke 12:34

"Again, the kingdom of heaven is like unto treasure hid in a field; the which when a man hath found, he

hideth, and for joy thereof goeth and selleth all that he hath, and buyeth that field."
Matthew 13:44

"Jesus said unto him, If thou wilt be perfect, go and sell that thou hast, and give to the poor, and thou shalt have treasure in heaven: and come and follow me."
Matthew 19:21

"No man can serve two masters: for either he will hate the one, and love the other; or else he will hold to the one, and despise the other. Ye cannot serve God and mammon."
Matthew 6:24

Notes:

8

The Airplane in Grandpa's Driveway

It was around 1960 when one of my uncles learned to fly an airplane. He was only sixteen years old and still living at home.

Having a license to fly an airplane is akin to having a license to drive a car; one feels the need of owning his own car or airplane. To that end, my uncle made a deal and purchased an old military trainer airplane that was disassembled for overhaul and restoration. In short, it would not fly without a lot of work being put into it.

Once you garner ownership of a car or an airplane you have to find a place to park it. Cars are easy enough, but airplanes are a different matter...they belong at the airport. This airplane was disassembled in pieces so my uncle decided to bring it home. I don't know if he consulted my Grandpa first or not about his plans.

I remember the main body of the airplane was parked on its wheels in the driveway. In the garage were the wings, the engine, the propeller, and some other random parts. Parts of the plane were painted blue and yellow so it was unmistakable what belonged on this contraption with an ancestry all the way back to the Wright Brothers.

Another twist to this story is that my grandparents had a large family and we were always visiting their house. The cousins always had a great time playing outside. We would also play on the airplane parked in the driveway. We took turns in the cockpit pretending to do our preflight, then start the engine (we had to make our own engine sounds), then take off into the wild blue yonder of our imagination.

For the cousins the airplane was just another stimulus for play, but for my grandpa it was an entirely different matter. This airplane had been parked in his driveway and filled his garage for five years. He had to live with that airplane every day, see it in the driveway every day, and his garage was useless to him. One day my grandpa had had enough, the time had come for action.

He tied that airplane to the back of his pickup and pulled it to the city dump. Everything went...the plane, the wings, the engine...everything. Finally, no airplane in the driveway. Grandpa had freedom at last!

My job as Pastor of First Baptist Church in Roxton is to point people toward Jesus Christ, the Son of God. Jesus has told us that we should not be burdened with the things of this world. What's amazing is when we focus our energy on Him things really come into perspective.

"Come unto me, all of you that labor and are heavy laden, and I will give you rest. Take my yoke upon you, and learn of me; for I am meek and lowly in heart: and ye shall find rest unto your souls. For my yoke is easy, and my burden is light."

Matthew 11:28-30

Even though my grandpa had a real airplane in his driveway, we humans have ways of parking other *airplanes* in the driveway of our lives. These *airplanes* can be almost anything: greed, selfishness, anger, jealousy and hatred, just to name a few. All of these things encumber our lives and prevent our relationship with God. The question remains then, when will you decide that you have had enough of the *airplane* consuming your life and get rid of it.

So if you have an *airplane* in your driveway, take it to Jesus and leave it with Him. After that you won't have to deal with it anymore, and you will be free.

Additional Scriptures

"Cast thy burden upon the Lord, and he shall sustain thee: he shall never suffer the righteous to be moved."
Psalm 55:22

"Stand fast therefore in the liberty wherewith Christ hath made us free, and be not entangled again with the yoke of bondage."
Galatians 5:1

"Now the Lord is that Spirit: and where the Spirit of the Lord is, there is liberty."
II Corinthians 3:17

"If the Son therefore shall make you free, ye shall be free indeed."
John 8:36

"And ye shall know the truth, and the truth shall make you free."
John 8:32

"I called upon the LORD in distress: the LORD answered me, and set me in a large place."
Psalm 118:5

Notes:

9

The Day I Left School

I suppose I have some of my Grandpa Holt's DNA that was passed on to me thru my mother. Grandpa was a man of action, and at an early age I too learned to take action.

I was in the first grade at Travis Elementary in Grand Prairie, Texas, and endured the day like most 6 year old boys. As long as the teacher kept me busy I was all right. When things got boring my DNA heritage from my grandpa would kick in.

One day we returned to our room from lunch and the teacher was delayed getting back. None of us knew where she was, so we patiently waited for her to return. After a while I figured I had waited long enough so I decided to leave...and leave I did.

We lived about three neighborhood blocks on Hickory Street, not too far from the school and I knew the trail like the back of my hand. I remember the day being clear and bright and navigating my way home was not a problem...until I got home. Mom wasn't there, she was at church.

We went to a new Baptist church in town, Baptist Temple, and my parents were actively engaged whenever possible. It so happened that the ladies had a daytime visitation program telling people about God's redemptive plan and asking them to come to our church.

When I discovered that Mom wasn't home that DNA kicked in again, and I concluded that the best thing to do was to return to the school.

In the meantime my teacher had returned to the classroom only to discover that I was not in my place. "Where's Louis?" she inquired. To her dismay no one in the class knew where I was. She ran to the office to get the Principal and the search was on. They went to my house only to discover I wasn't there. My teacher left a note on the door telling my Mom to contact her when she got home.

Somehow with the neighborhood *All Points Bulletin* out on me I eluded their search. I calmly moseyed my way back to the school, to my classroom, and back to my desk. As far as I was concerned all was well. Not so with my teacher and the Principal.

I guess they covered a search radius a bored 6 year old boy might travel but to no avail. My teacher returned to the classroom only to find me calmly sitting at my desk. I don't recall any repercussions from my afternoon adventure; all must have been too relieved that I was safe.

Sometimes I think Christian people lose patience waiting on God to *come into the room* and decide to wander off on their own. We all have issues in our lives and there are times we want God to take action *right now*. We forget that God is sovereign, meaning that God always takes action in HIS time, not ours. The old song, "Trust and Obey," could not be truer. We must learn to trust God and obey God. We must also learn patience as part of trusting in Him.

"Be still and know that I am God."
Psalm 46:10

Even the Patriarchs of the Bible had to learn to trust God and wait on his provision. Noah was powerless to control the ark he built at God's command, only God could steer the vessel to safety in the storms. Moses was powerless against the Egyptians, only God could free the children of Israel from Egyptian bondage. Daniel was powerless against the lions in the den, only God could shut the mouths of those beasts. All these are examples of God working His Sovereign will in His Sovereign way in his Sovereign time.

We too are powerless on our own against the devil as he roams the earth as a roaring lion seeking whom he may devour. So be patient. Wait on God. He will come into the room.

Additional Scriptures

"He that is slow to wrath is of great understanding: but he that is hasty of spirit exalteth folly."
Proverbs 14:29

"Be kindly affectioned one to another with brotherly love; in honour preferring one another; 11 Not slothful in business; fervent in spirit; serving the

Lord; 12 Rejoicing in hope; patient in tribulation; continuing instant in prayer; 13 Distributing to the necessity of saints; given to hospitality. 14 Bless them which persecute you: bless, and curse not. 15 Rejoice with them that do rejoice, and weep with them that weep.
Romans 12:10-15

"Rest in the LORD, and wait patiently for him: fret not thyself because of him who prospereth in his way, because of the man who bringeth wicked devices to pass."
Psalm 37:7

"The Lord is not slack concerning his promise, as some men count slackness; but is longsuffering to us-ward, not willing that any should perish, but that all should come to repentance."
II Peter 3:9

"The LORD is merciful and gracious, slow to anger, and plenteous in mercy."
Psalm 103:8

"But, beloved, be not ignorant of this one thing, that one day is with the Lord as a thousand years, and a thousand years as one day."
II Peter 3:8

Notes:

10

The Value of a Mentor – Part One

I have been fortunate to have mentors along the way in my life. A mentor is like a teacher or a guide. A mentor could also be thought of as a trusted advisor. Some of my mentors were young men, but most were old men. I've even had a couple of elderly ladies pass along sound words of wisdom. I cherish them all and I'm so thankful they were there.

One of my earliest mentors was a gentle old man we called Grandpa Richardson. He was a member of our church and lived close by just across a small field. As a young boy I never learned his first name, so I called him Grandpa Richardson.

Frequently after school I would make the short trek to his apartment for a visit. One of the first pleasures he taught me about was the joy of a cold Dr Pepper and ginger snap cookies. Back in those days our Dr Pepper came in small glass bottles and was made with real sugar. I remember the flavors were bold and exciting. Then we would sit at the table and play Chinese checkers. We also played regular checkers. I think he let me win most of the time but it was always great fun to be there.

Grandpa Richardson would go to flea markets a lot during the day and he would always show me the latest treasures he bought, usually a watch or perhaps an old guitar or banjo. He would play the guitar or banjo for me and ask me to guess the name of the song. Now his fingers were stiff with arthritis so he was not able to fret the instrument at all. He would strum the instrument with a rhythmic drone for a while and ask me to guess the name of the song. Even though I didn't have a clue what he was playing I would listen attentively and smile then make the best guess I could. I always got it wrong. I don't think he minded because he had a small boy to give him some attention and pass the day with another cold Dr Pepper and a handful of ginger snaps.

There were a couple of occasions where the church that my dad pastored would add on to the church building. Men of the church would all chip in as they cut and nailed the boards together. Grandpa Richardson was not one to be left out when there is work to be done. Since his apartment was just across the field from the church he would grab his cane and come to the job site.

Grandpa Richardson took on the toughest job of anyone...he would clean up the area where the work was being done. He would pick up trash and would also pull nails out of scrap boards so the boards could be used again. He managed to obtain one of those long nail bars that made it easy to pull the nails.

My dad made photographic records of the work done at the church and in most pictures Grandpa Richardson is standing there in his big hat, working just as hard as anyone else.

The Bible makes reference to mentoring in several places, one is found in Proverbs.

"Iron sharpeneth iron; so a man sharpeneth the countenance of his friend."
Proverbs 27:17

Mentoring begins by building a friendship!
Another verse on mentoring is in Proverbs 20:

"The glory of young men is their strength: and the beauty of old men is the gray head."
Proverbs 20:29

While a young man might be strong he has yet to season his life with wisdom. It's the wisdom that makes an old man beautiful. Wisdom needs to be shared.

Grandpa Richardson taught me to enjoy simple pleasures, to fill my life with music, and the value of honest work. Now that I am older I trust I'm earning my gray head too. I hope that makes me beautiful like Grandpa Richardson.

Additional Scriptures

"And the things that thou hast heard of me among many witnesses, the same commit thou to faithful men, who shall be able to teach others also."
II Timothy 2:2

"Train up a child in the way he should go: and when he is old, he will not depart from it."
Proverbs 22:6

"Now also when I am old and greyheaded, O God, forsake me not; until I have shewed thy strength unto this generation, and thy power to every one that is to come."
Psalm 71:18

"A wise man will hear, and will increase learning; and a man of understanding shall attain unto wise counsels:"
Proverbs 1:5

"But the Comforter, which is the Holy Ghost, whom the Father will send in my name, he shall teach you all things, and bring all things to your remembrance, whatsoever I have said unto you."
John 14:26

"He that walketh with wise men shall be wise: but a companion of fools shall be destroyed."
Proverbs 13:20

Notes:

11

The Value of a Mentor – Part Two

One time my Dad's church in Grapevine was invited to attend a revival meeting at another church in town. We obliged and went.

Upon arrival the folks in my Dad's church greeted the folks at the other church then my Dad's church sat all together in the auditorium. When it was time to sing, we sang as best we could. When it was time to pray, we prayed for the working of the Holy Spirit. When it was time for the preaching the evangelist asked everyone in attendance to hold up their Bible. Everyone in my Dad's church had their Bible. We all raised them high into the air as instructed. There were only a couple of Bibles that were raised in the hosting church. One elderly lady that was visiting the hosting church herself took notice of what just happened.

The following Sunday that lady came to my Dad's church for services. At the altar call she came forward and joined my dad's church on the spot! She said she wanted to be part of a church that really believed the Bible. She was impressed that we all had our Bibles with us at the revival.

I took a shining to Mrs. Daley. She was always glad to see me and had a genuine interest in how my life was progressing. What was really neat to me is that it did not matter what we talked about, she would encourage me with Scriptures from the Bible.

This great woman really knew her Bible. She could quote scripture and make application no matter the situation.

The Bible speaks of what an elderly woman can and should do.

"The aged women likewise, that they be in behaviour as becometh holiness, not false accusers, not given to much wine, teachers of good things; 4 That they may teach the young women to be sober, to love their husbands, to love their children, 5 To be discreet, chaste, keepers at home, good, obedient to their own husbands, that the word of God be not blasphemed."
Titus 2:3-5

Then we have verse 6 which states:

"Young men likewise exhort to be sober minded."

We need grandmothers and great-grandmothers to stand up and teach their granddaughters and grandsons these essential Biblical truths...to be temperate, chaste, modest, moderate, wise, and prudent in all things. That's sound practical teaching for a productive life, wouldn't you agree?

I adopted Mrs. Daley as my own. I might not have been the sharpest knife in the drawer but I knew a good thing when I saw it. I was drawn to the loving interest she had for me. I gladly sat and listened as she would reveal the Word of God every time I visited with her.

Mrs. Daley taught me the value of putting the Word of God in my heart and life. She read the Word, memorized the Word, and she spread the Word.

Notice these words from the Psalmist:

"Thy Word have I hid in mine heart, that I might not sin against Thee."
Psalm 119:11

Mrs. Daley lived it.

Finally, Mrs. Daley taught me the joy of unselfish living. It takes time to read and memorize the Bible. She unselfishly spent the time in order that she could mentor a preacher's son that desperately needed to hear what God had for me.

I hope you have found this an encouragement to take a young boy or girl and be a mentor to them. I believe that with honest interest in them and giving them the precepts in the Bible that we can make a difference in their lives.

So have them turn off the television and put away the video games so you can spend valuable time with them. Children are our heritage and blessing. Play with them, read to them, and talk to them, and pray for them. For once really make a difference.

Additional Scriptures

"Hear, O Israel: The LORD our God is one LORD: 5 And thou shalt love the LORD thy God with all thine heart, and with all thy soul, and with all thy might. 6 And these words, which I command thee this day, shall be in thine heart: 7 And thou shalt teach them diligently unto thy children, and shalt talk of them when thou sittest in thine house, and when thou walkest by the way, and when thou liest down, and when thou risest up. 8 And thou shalt bind them for a sign upon thine hand, and they shall be as frontlets between thine eyes. 9 And thou shalt write them upon the posts of thy house, and on thy gates."
Deuteronomy 6:4-9

"The entrance of thy words giveth light; it giveth understanding unto the simple."
Psalm 119:130

"I opened my mouth, and panted: for I longed for thy commandments"
Psalm 119:131

"Let no man despise thy youth; but be thou an example of the believers, in word, in conversation, in charity, in spirit, in faith, in purity."
I Timothy 4:12

"If any of you lack wisdom, let him ask of God, that giveth to all men liberally, and upbraideth not; and it shall be given him."
James 1:5

"My little children, these things write I unto you, that ye sin not."
I John 2:1a

Notes:

12

The Life of a Bug

The greatest treasure given to mankind is the Word of God, the Bible. In it is God's revelation of Himself to man, His redemptive plan for man, and God's judgement of man in the end times.

It was A. T. Pierson that called the Bible, "God's Living Oracle." His book by the same name was published in 1904. It is available on the internet and worth the read.

Now I know what you're thinking, what does the Bible have to do with the life of a bug? It's because the Bible is completely accurate and true in all things, including bugs!

The Bible tells us in Genesis chapter one that God created bugs on the sixth day of creation.

"And God said, Let the earth bring forth the living creature after his kind, cattle, and creeping thing, and beast of the earth after his kind: and it was so."
Genesis 1:24

God created bugs, *creeping things*, on the sixth day. He also created all manner of beast, including lions, tigers, bears, skunks, armadillos, and last but not least, the dinosaurs.

The Bible also tells us that God is omniscient, meaning He is all knowing. That said, God has been, and always will be aware of the life of every creature that has ever lived, including the bug.

Bugs come in all varieties, colors, sizes, and configurations. I believe that God took great pleasure in His creative ability when He made the bugs. God knew some men would be fascinated by these amazing creatures so He freely created all kinds of bugs. Red bugs, green bugs, gray bugs, black bugs. Big bugs, small bugs, jumping bugs, walking bugs, flying bugs. Noisy bugs, quiet bugs, singing bugs, chirping bugs. Big bugs, little bugs, long bugs, short bugs. All kinds of bugs, each created for the glory of God!

I believe that God knows when each bug is hatched and when each bug dies. Every bug has its purpose to glorify God, all ordained of God.

God created the heaven and the Earth first, and everything that God created was for the Earth and the life that He placed upon it.

"Thou sendest forth thy spirit, they are created:"
Psalm 104:30

The scientific community would have us believe that bugs evolved over millions of years. According to the Word of God, bugs were created instantly in all their infinite varieties on the sixth day of creation.

If you drive your car on a summer evening you will most likely have your windshield spattered with bugs. You will, in vain, try the windshield washer to remove the residue of the bugs. You will discover your wipers are worn out, or your washer fluid is empty, or most likely discover that your windshield washer fluid is ineffective at removing the bugs. That's just the risk of driving on a summers evening.

But just ponder on this; that God is aware of every bug that gave its life on your windshield, and personally, I'm glad that He is. It is another reminder that God is exactly who He says He is, the Sovereign of the Universe. He is all-powerful, all-knowing, ever-present, holy, wise, and just. He is the God of creation. He is the God of Abraham, Isaac, and Jacob. He is a covenant keeping God. He is faithful and true.

If God is mindful of the bug, just think how much He is mindful of you.

Additional Scriptures

"Go to the ant, thou sluggard; consider her ways, and be wise: 7 Which having no guide, overseer, or ruler, 8 Provideth her meat in the summer, and gathereth her food in the harvest."
Proverbs 6:6-8

"And after a time he returned to take her, and he turned aside to see the carcase of the lion: and, behold, there was a swarm of bees and honey in the carcase of the lion."
Judges 14:8

"The locusts have no king, yet go they forth all of them by bands;"
Proverbs 30:27

"The spider taketh hold with her hands, and is in kings' palaces."
Proverbs 30:28

"It is he that sitteth upon the circle of the earth, and the inhabitants thereof are as grasshoppers; that stretcheth out the heavens as a curtain, and spreadeth them out as a tent to dwell in:"
Isaiah 40:22

"But lay up for yourselves treasures in heaven, where neither moth nor rust doth corrupt, and where thieves do not break through nor steal:"
Matthew 6:20

Notes:

13

Find a Penny, Pick it Up

Sometimes I think people must throw pennies away; they are simply everywhere. Every time I see one I pick it up.

I was at an early age when I learned the value of a penny. Two blocks away from our house in Grapevine was a convenience store that would give me two pennies for each empty soda pop bottle I returned. Anytime I needed to increase my cash supply I would scour the house and garage for empty pop bottles. Five bottles would translate into a silver dime. It was a real bonanza in those days.

Benjamin Franklin said, "A penny saved is a penny earned." Words never rang more true. There are many ways to save that penny, but simply spending less is the easiest. Many folks live on the financial edge due to spending rather than saving what they earn.

If I see that unmistakable copper coin on the ground I will pick it up. Five of them make a nickel and ten will make a dime. When I pick up the next coin I am another penny richer. I pick them up because they are valuable to me.

Truth is like a penny; it is everywhere. God in His infinite wisdom has shown us His truth for our benefit.

"For the LORD is good; his mercy is everlasting; and his truth endures to all generations."
Psalm 100:5

And just like a penny, the truth is there; all we have to do is pick it up. Occasionally I will come across another truth revealed by God. Just like the penny, I waste no time in picking it up and acquiring it for my life. It is valuable to me.

Finally, in the Bible there is a passage that I wish every young person knew. It's a nugget of golden truth for life, found in Proverbs chapter 3.

"Let not mercy and truth forsake thee: bind them about thy neck; write them upon the table of thine heart: 4 So shalt thou find favour and good understanding in the sight of God and man. 5 Trust in the Lord with all thine heart; and lean not unto thine own understanding. 6 In all thy ways acknowledge him, and he shall direct thy paths."
Proverbs 3:3-6

I hope now that you parents and grand-parents will pass this truth along to your children.

In verse 3, it not only mentions truth, but mercy as well. Mercy is simply goodness bestowed on those in misery or distress. In other words, be kind to those around you. Like truth, mercy goes a long way when applied.

I hope the next time you see truth that you will pick it up and hold fast to it. To borrow from

Benjamin Franklin, "A truth saved is a truth earned." Embrace it. Apply it. Never let it go.

Additional Scriptures

"Lying lips are abomination to the LORD: but they that deal truly are his delight."
Proverbs 12:22

"Therefore I love thy commandments above gold; yea, above fine gold."
Psalm 119:127

"And we know that the Son of God is come, and hath given us an understanding, that we may know him that is true, and we are in him that is true, even in his Son Jesus Christ. This is the true God, and eternal life."
I John 5:20

"My little children, let us not love in word, neither in tongue; but in deed and in truth."
I John 3:18

"He that walketh uprightly, and worketh righteousness, and speaketh the truth in his heart. 3 He that backbiteth not with his tongue, nor doeth evil to his neighbour, nor taketh up a reproach against his neighbour."
Psalm 15:2-3

"Again, the kingdom of heaven is like unto treasure hid in a field; the which when a man hath found, he hideth, and for joy thereof goeth and selleth all that he hath, and buyeth that field."
Matthew 13:44
Notes:

14

A Conversation with a Laughing Gull

I had been looking forward to this for a long time; a warm breeze, sandy beaches, and blue waters. This vacation was timely and desperately needed. No longer than I had setup my chair on the beach at Padre Island to sit in the sun and relax, when I begin to hear this hilarious laughter. The laughter continued and got louder. When I looked behind me to see it, there was a flock of Laughing Gulls that had joined our day camp on the beach.

Over the years people on the beach have been feeding these birds so when they see humans they approach and beg for a meal. Jan and I did not feed them, but during the day at the beach I had the opportunity to observe and learn about this remarkable bird.

The Laughing Gull is named because it sounds like it is laughing. It is quite realistic as it goes, *"Hah, ha, ha, ha, ha, hah, hah, hah."* Their heads bob up and down and sometimes they look up to the sky as they conclude their laugh with the last "hah." They will laugh as they perch on the ground. They will laugh as they fly. They will do acrobatics in front of you to get attention and then go into their laugh once again.

God, in His wisdom, created this bird for His glory. The Laughing Gull is doing exactly as God commanded it; be fruitful and multiply. They reverence the Creator God with their obedience to His command. To that end, their day is spent doing what birds do best; looking for food and mating.

One of the first things I noticed is that when the birds perch on the ground they always face into the wind. While we were on the beach the winds were quite brisk out of the south so when the gulls perched on the ground they always faced south. Even on the ground their bodies are very aerodynamic. We noticed several birds that would perch on one foot and preen their feathers, all while facing into the wind. If they decided to fly, they would simply spread their wings and take a couple of steps forward and they would effortlessly lift into the air.

Another thing I noticed is that several birds were missing a foot or the entire leg. They would perch on their one foot, fly from a one foot hop into the air, and gently land on one foot. Even though they were what we would perceive as handicapped, they did not act like they were handicapped. They continued to do what God wanted them to do; be fruitful and multiply. (There's a lesson in that.)

If only *man* were as willing to give glory to God as the Laughing Gull. Instead, men are pursuing their own will, doing that which they desire to do. It is rare to find a person that will consider counselling in order to live a victorious life. If they would simply consider the Laughing Gull they could learn much.

"The way of a fool is right in his own eyes: but he that listens unto counsel is wise."
Proverbs 12:15

King Solomon summed it up in the book of Ecclesiastes:

"Fear God, and keep his commandments: for this is the whole duty of man."
Ecclesiastes 12:13b

The word *fear* in this verse could be the same as *reverence*. The LORD God is truly great in might and power, and also great in the way that He loves each of us.

So if you don't believe me, believe the Laughing Gull. He would tell you the same thing!

Additional Scriptures

"20 And God said, Let the waters bring forth abundantly the moving creature that hath life, and fowl that may fly above the earth in the open firmament of heaven. 21 And God created great whales, and every living creature that moveth, which the waters brought forth abundantly, after their kind, and every winged fowl after his kind: and God saw that it was good. 22 And God blessed them, saying, Be fruitful, and multiply, and fill the waters in the seas, and let fowl multiply in the earth."

Genesis 1:20-22

"But ask now the beasts, and they shall teach thee; and the fowls of the air, and they shall tell thee: 8 Or speak to the earth, and it shall teach thee: and the fishes of the sea shall declare unto thee. 9 Who knoweth not in all these that the hand of the LORD hath wrought this? 10 In whose hand is the soul of every living thing, and the breath of all mankind."
Job 12:7-10

"Behold the fowls of the air: for they sow not, neither do they reap, nor gather into barns; yet your heavenly Father feedeth them. Are ye not much better than they?"
Matthew 6:26

"He giveth to the beast his food, and to the young ravens which cry."
Psalm 147:9

"Let them praise the name of the LORD: for he commanded, and they were created. 6 He hath also stablished them for ever and ever: he hath made a decree which shall not pass. 7 Praise the LORD from the earth, ye dragons, and all deeps: 8 Fire, and hail; snow, and vapours; stormy wind fulfilling his word: 9 Mountains, and all hills; fruitful trees, and all cedars: 10 Beasts, and all cattle; creeping things, and flying fowl:
Psalm 148:5-10

"Are not five sparrows sold for two farthings, and not one of them is forgotten before God?"
Luke 12:6

Notes:

15

I Know Who Holds Tomorrow

We live with much uncertainty these days. It seems that planet Earth is out of control as we listen to the evening news broadcast. The things we used to trust in have become unstable for our families. The stock markets, government, politicians, war, terrorism, the agenda of special interest groups, all seem to overwhelm us every day.

Who then can we turn to and in whom can we trust?

Wouldn't it be nice to be able to depend upon someone that is greater than the upheaval of this world? And this someone would be there no matter where you are in your life. Wouldn't it be nice to know that there could be perfect peace and harmony deep within your soul?

Well, I don't know about tomorrow, no one on this earth does, but I know who holds tomorrow.

It was Joshua who had just taken command of Israel and the future seemed uncertain. There were people to care for and a land to be conquered. God met him with these words in the book of Joshua:

"Have not I commanded thee? Be strong and of a good courage; be not afraid, neither be thou dismayed: for the LORD thy God is with thee whithersoever thou go."
Joshua 1:9

Joshua was over 80 years old, yet he accomplished the task and God took care of him. We have to remember that when God commands, He will always follow through as He said.

Like many others, I too have chosen to place my confidence in God. Through the years I have witnessed His goodness and mercy in my life and in the lives of others. It was the psalmist that wrote in Psalm 16:

"I have set the LORD always before me: because he is at my right hand, I shall not be moved.
9 Therefore my heart is glad, and my glory rejoiceth: my flesh also shall rest in hope."
Psalm 16:8-9

The thought here is that David kept the LORD before him, meaning that no matter what came his way he always placed his confidence in God. For David, knowing God was a way of life. Further, David said that God is at his right hand, or in other words, God is always present with him. No wonder David wrote about the joy that he had!

In verse 11 David further wrote:

"Thou wilt shew me the path of life: in thy presence is fulness of joy; at thy right hand there are pleasures for evermore."
Psalm 16:11

It was David's son Solomon that wrote in Proverbs chapter 3:

"5 Trust in the LORD with all thine heart; and lean not unto thine own understanding. 6 In all thy ways acknowledge him, and he shall direct thy paths."
Proverbs 3:5-6

Happiness and joy are the results of trusting God for direction in our lives, both for today and tomorrow. We can then navigate life with confidence and the knowledge of Him. When the world is spinning out of control, the stock market fails, unemployment looms, or we struggle with sickness and death, we have the confidence and joy deep inside our soul that can only come from God.

It was songwriter Ira F. Stanphill who wrote these great lyrics:

"Many things about tomorrow
I don't seem to understand
But I know who holds tomorrow
And I know who holds my hand."

The eternal peace and joy of God is there for you; it always has been and always will be. Whether or not you embrace Him is your choice. I hope you will; then you too will know who holds tomorrow.

Additional Scriptures

"13 Go to now, ye that say, Today or tomorrow we will go into such a city, and continue there a year, and buy and sell, and get gain: 14 Whereas ye know not what shall be on the morrow. For what is your life? It is even a vapour, that appeareth for a little time, and then vanisheth away. 15 For that ye ought to say, If the Lord will, we shall live, and do this, or that."
James 4:13-15

"Beloved, now are we the sons of God, and it doth not yet appear what we shall be: but we know that, when he shall appear, we shall be like him; for we shall see him as he is."
I John 3:2

"Let not your heart be troubled: ye believe in God, believe also in me. 2 In my Father's house are many mansions: if it were not so, I would have told you. I go to prepare a place for you. 3 And if I go and prepare a place for you, I will come again, and receive you unto myself; that where I am, there ye may be also."
John 14:1-3

"Boast not thyself of tomorrow; for thou knowest not what a day may bring forth."
Proverbs 27:1

"The fear of the LORD prolongeth days: but the years of the wicked shall be shortened."

Proverbs 10:27

"He that regardeth the day, regardeth it unto the Lord; and he that regardeth not the day, to the Lord he doth not regard it. He that eateth, eateth to the Lord, for he giveth God thanks; and he that eateth not, to the Lord he eateth not, and giveth God thanks."
Romans 14:6

Notes:

16

Of Things You Have Only One

I have always heard it said that a cat has nine lives. It's a saying that's been around for a long time. "With three he will play, with three he will stray, and with three he will stay," so the saying goes.

The domestic housecat is truly an amazing creation of God. Cats have this incredible ability to right themselves in a fall. There are countless stories where cats have fallen from high places and landed on their feet. Other stories where they narrowly escape danger with lightning fast reflexes. While the myth continues to this day, reality dictates that a cat has only one life.

And like the cat, you too only have one life.

Many people feel invincible, but they are not. People die every day attempting to do something dangerous; feeling that they will not be hurt.

The Bible tells us:

"And as it is appointed unto men once to die, but after this the judgment:"
Hebrews 9:27

So there are two certainties here to deal with: death and judgement by God.

The question then is since you have only one life, what will you do with it? I heard some comments by Clayton Christensen where he discussed the fact that God keeps detailed records of your life, so when your judgement day comes all evidence will be presented. I believe that God will ask you the question, "What did you do with your life?"

The Bible gives us guidance of what to do. Jesus was approached by a very religious man who happened to be a lawyer and he asked Jesus a question. Jesus' answer is the cornerstone of what you should do with your life. In Matthew is the detailed account:

"36 Master, which is the great commandment in the law? 37 Jesus said unto him, Thou shalt love the Lord thy God with all thy heart, and with all thy soul, and with all thy mind. 38 This is the first and great commandment. 39 And the second is like unto it, Thou shalt love thy neighbor as thyself. 40 On these two commandments hang all the law and the prophets."
Matthew 22:36-40

I encourage the people at First Baptist in Roxton to read their Bible every day. "Why," you might ask. It's because it is the Word of God that reveals God to us. The more we know about God the more we love Him. And the more we love Him the easier it is to love our neighbor.

Your neighbors are the people that live in the community where you live, beginning with the folks in the house next door. Your neighbor can also be someone you work with every day, someone you go to school with every day. Your neighbor is the next customer that comes into your store, the person that goes to the community food pantry to get their next meal. Your neighbor is that person that might look different than you with a different shade of skin or different shaped eyes.

When the day comes and we stand before God I believe that the all-knowing, omniscient God will do a thorough examination of our lives. He will have all the records, each detail will be accurate, and nothing will be held back. All of heaven will be attentive as each detail is presented as evidence.

You have only one life to live. Start today by honoring God and loving your neighbor. It will all be for the good.

Additional Scriptures

"And as it is appointed unto men once to die, but after this the judgment:"
Hebrews 9:27

"For the poor shall never cease out of the land: therefore I command thee, saying, Thou shalt open thine hand wide unto thy brother, to thy poor, and to thy needy, in thy land."
Deuteronomy 15:11

"Give to him that asketh thee, and from him that would borrow of thee turn not thou away."
Matthew 5:42

"For I was an hungred, and ye gave me meat: I was thirsty, and ye gave me drink: I was a stranger, and ye took me in: 36 Naked, and ye clothed me: I was sick, and ye visited me: I was in prison, and ye came unto me."
Matthew 25:35-36

"Sell that ye have, and give alms; provide yourselves bags which wax not old, a treasure in the heavens that faileth not, where no thief approacheth, neither moth corrupteth."
Luke 12:33

"Heal the sick, cleanse the lepers, raise the dead, cast out devils: freely ye have received, freely give."
Matthew 10:8

Notes:

17

Wildflowers and Sunsets

It was the spring of 1963 when the most wonderful thing happened...my sister Jeanne and I learned about wildflowers and sunsets.

It was the fall of 1962 when my dad accepted the pastorate of Bethel Baptist Church in Grapevine, TX and we moved into the parsonage behind the church. Now, the parsonage was a small, unfinished house with no carpet, no central heat, and no air conditioning. That first winter was cold. I remember staying close to the Dearborn heater most all the time.

Since the parsonage was behind the church the view from our front door wasn't that good; we could see the unremarkable rear of the church building and a muddy parking lot. The view from the back door wasn't any good either with only a fence and weeds. There was a rent house just to our east and a field of weeds on a hill sloping down to the west. It was kind of a boxed in feeling if you know what I mean. Then spring came and the most remarkable thing happened.

The view from the front door was the same, as was the view to the north behind the parsonage, and the rent house was still to the east. It was the view to the west that changed.

The lady that owned the property to our west never mowed so the flora just grew wild. And mixed in was the most beautiful patch of Bluebonnets and Indian Paintbrushes. The blue and the orange were overwhelming. There were also other wildflowers mixed in, but the Bluebonnets and Paintbrushes were the main attraction. My sister and I were taken in with the view, discovering something remarkable and new.

Dad owned a 35mm camera and he took pictures of the wildflowers. To this day it is still a joy to see those pictures and the memories they bring. Dad also took pictures of the sunsets with stunning displays of clouds over orange, yellow, and red color from the sun. I suppose that God knew we needed something extraordinary in the way of a blessing, and the wildflowers and sunsets did the trick. I had learned to appreciate the beauty of God's marvelous creation. After that I looked forward to the next spring of 1964 to see the wildflowers and sunsets again.

We must remember that God made all of creation for His glory. The Bluebonnets and Indian Paintbrushes praise the Creator in their beauty. Even the sunsets are orchestrated by God in infinite splendor so that we might see His glory.

"Thou, even thou, art LORD alone; thou hast made heaven, the heaven of heavens, with all their host, the earth, and all things that are therein, the seas, and all that is therein, and thou preservest them all; and the host of heaven worships thee."
Nehemiah 9:6

In His infinite knowledge God knew that in the year 1963, or about 5,963 years after the creative week, that an 8 year old boy and a 4 year old girl and their parents would need a blessing. And there it was just to the west of our house...beautiful wildflowers and stunning sunsets. God created them just for us.

Additional Scriptures

"The grass withereth, the flower fadeth: but the word of our God shall stand for ever."
Isaiah 40:8

"Consider the lilies how they grow: they toil not, they spin not; and yet I say unto you, that Solomon in all his glory was not arrayed like one of these."
Luke 12:27

"He maketh me to lie down in green pastures: he leadeth me beside the still waters. 3 He restoreth my soul: he leadeth me in the paths of righteousness for his name's sake."
Psalm 23:2-3

"They also that dwell in the uttermost parts are afraid at thy tokens: thou makest the outgoings of the morning and evening to rejoice."
Psalm 65:8

"From the rising of the sun unto the going down of the same the LORD's name is to be praised."
Psalm 113:3

"For as the heaven is high above the earth, so great is his mercy toward them that fear him. 12 As far as the east is from the west, so far hath he removed our transgressions from us."
Psalm 103:11-12

Notes:

18

A Big Pill to Swallow

When my dad went into the ministry in 1962 at Bethel Baptist Church in Grapevine, it was a huge adjustment for the entire family. The ministry is a different way of life where all the family members are involved in one way or another. Preachers' kids feel the stresses of the ministry as well and I was no exception.

I remember a few times where I dealt with stomach issues and would simply get sick. Looking back now, it was probably induced more by nerves than anything else. There were times when dad would take me to the doctor feeling there was nothing else he could do.

Dad used an old doctor in town who was retired from the military. This old doctor did not charge preachers for his services. He was also a cartoonist with his bizarre drawings on the wall in his examination room. This old doctor was fond of penicillin and his usual diagnosis would include an injection in the hip with this wonder drug. I became really afraid to go to this doctor because I knew what would happen...a shot in the hip.

On one occasion Dad took me to this old doctor and I really put up a fuss. In my mind this doctor was the meanest man on the planet. And there is more...there was the sounds of horror in my mind of him fetching the penicillin from the refrigerator in the next room, then the clank of assembly of the glass syringe from the steam sterilizer located behind the examination table. As I heard the sounds in the office the horror captivated my mind and I cried and begged for mercy. Then the most wonderful thing happened.

This crusty old doctor made a deal with me. He said that if I could swallow a big pill I would not have to take a shot. For me it was a euphoria of relief, but, the euphoria was short lived. This old doctor walked in with a capsule that was huge, and I mean huge. It was about an inch in diameter and about 3 inches long. I looked at that capsule in astonishment knowing that the difficulties of swallowing it couldn't be any worse that an injection from that obviously dull needle.

All of a sudden the doctor and my Dad broke out into laughter. Come to find out, the pill was a joke. I really did not have to swallow it. The pill was part of an advertising campaign for a drug company. The pill itself was hollow and just for show. Even better, I did not have to take a shot either. Now I was laughing!

Sometimes I think that people avoid church for the same reasons I wanted to avoid this old doctor. They associate God and religion with uncomfortable feelings and perceived pain from enduring the religious experience.

Perhaps the biggest pill to swallow is the idea of coming to terms with God Himself. I find that many people's perceptions about God come from what someone else has told them or what they have seen in the movies or other media. Fortunately, these perceptions are not true. God is not a bumbling old man in the clouds that doesn't have a clue of what's going on.

The Bible tells us that God is the all-knowing, all powerful, ever present God that desires the best for us. He knows each of us by name not to mention that He knows everything about you and your life. God truly cares for you, even desiring that you would bring all your burdens and cares to Him. The Bible says that God loves you with a love that our human minds cannot comprehend.

Most of all, God desires for you to live eternally in heaven with Him. Just think, the Creator and Sovereign of the Universe is thinking of you.

Finally, The Bible sums up the Gospel in one passage found in John chapter 3 verse 16,

"For God so loved the world that he gave his only begotten Son that whosoever believeth in Him should not perish, but have everlasting life."

It's not really a big pill, all you have to do is believe.

Additional Scriptures

"But God commendeth his love toward us, in that, while we were yet sinners, Christ died for us."

Romans 5:8

"Neither is there salvation in any other: for there is none other name under heaven given among men, whereby we must be saved."
Acts 4:12

"Jesus answered, Verily, verily, I say unto thee, Except a man be born of water and of the Spirit, he cannot enter into the kingdom of God."
John 3:5

"Not every one that saith unto me, Lord, Lord, shall enter into the kingdom of heaven; but he that doeth the will of my Father which is in heaven."
Matthew 7:21

"Seek ye the LORD while he may be found, call ye upon him while he is near: 7 Let the wicked forsake his way, and the unrighteous man his thoughts: and let him return unto the LORD, and he will have mercy upon him; and to our God, for he will abundantly pardon."
Isaiah 55:6-7

"That if thou shalt confess with thy mouth the Lord Jesus, and shalt believe in thine heart that God hath raised him from the dead, thou shalt be saved. 10 For with the heart man believeth unto righteousness; and with the mouth confession is made unto salvation."

Romans 10:9-10

Notes:

19

The Love of the Father

My mother told me the story about when she was around 15 years old, my grandfather Holt had leased a large parcel of land and was raising a cotton crop. Back in those days all the able bodied children in the family would work in the fields. So it was that Mom and her younger brothers worked both in hoeing in summer, then later picking the cotton in the fall.

Apparently, Grandpa had a huge production going with his cotton crop as it was too much for the family to handle by themselves. So he hired additional workers to help get the crop in.

The days were long and hot. Mom said that the rows were so long, they were seemingly endless. Grandpa was mindful of his children and to that end would at times do something very special. On one occasion, he came by to check on the progress of the work, and brought little cups of ice-cream he had purchased at a country store near the field. He called his children to the end of the row, then gave each one a frozen cup of ice-cream with a little wooden spoon and allowed them to sit in the shade of the pick-up to enjoy their treat. I can imagine their delight as they savored every cold spoonful on such a hot day. My grandfather had done something very special for his children, but he did not buy ice-cream for the hired hands.

The Bible says in Malachi chapter 4 verse 17,

"And they shall be mine, saith the LORD of host, in that day when I make up my jewels; and I will spare them, as a man spareth his own son that serveth him."

I don't know if Grandpa knew of this verse or not but he followed its principles. He was not going to allow his children to work for him without special recognition or favor. They were his. He loved them and cared for them as they worked in his fields.

God the Father loves all people of the world, even those who are not His children. He always has since the beginning. The Bible says in John chapter 3 and verse 16,

"For God so loved the world, that he gave his only begotten Son, that whosoever believeth in him should not perish, but have everlasting life."

What a wondrous gift from the Heavenly Father to the people of the world. But for those who are unwilling to become his children they are paid the wages for their sin. Romans chapter 6 verse 23 explains this further;

"For the wages of sin is death; but the gift of God is eternal life through Jesus Christ our Lord."

The love of the Father is so great that He reminds the sinner once again that the gift of God is eternal life through Jesus!

My grandpa Holt went to live with Jesus in 1979. In his life he was a man of integrity and impeccable character. As he was mindful of my mother when she was a young girl working in his cotton fields, he was also mindful of me as his grandson. On numerous occasions he did special things for me, not only because I was his grandson, but because he was mentoring and teaching me the value of thoughtfulness and love.

For those of you who are fathers, be sure to be thoughtful of your children, showing them special favor and how you care for them above all else. In First John chapter 3 and verse 1a it says,

"Behold, what manner of love the Father hath bestowed upon us, that we should be called the sons of God."

You don't have to buy them a 400 dollar video game; a 79 cent cup of ice cream will do. Don't forget the wooden spoon.

Additional Scriptures

"But love ye your enemies, and do good, and lend, hoping for nothing again; and your reward shall be great, and ye shall be the children of the Highest: for he is kind unto the unthankful and to the evil. 36 Be ye therefore merciful, as your Father also is merciful.

Luke 6:35-36

"Behold, what manner of love the Father hath
bestowed upon us, that we should be called the sons of
God: therefore the world knoweth us not, because it
knew him not. 2 Beloved, now are we the sons of God,
and it doth not yet appear what we shall be: but we
know that, when he shall appear, we shall be like him;
for we shall see him as he is."
I John 3:1-2

"For ye have not received the spirit of bondage again to
fear; but ye have received the Spirit of adoption,
whereby we cry, Abba, Father. 16 The Spirit itself
beareth witness with our spirit, that we are the children
of God:"
Romans 8:15-16

"Fear not, little flock; for it is your Father's good
pleasure to give you the kingdom."
Luke 12:32

"Let not your heart be troubled: ye believe in God,
believe also in me."
John 14:1

"Behold the fowls of the air: for they sow not, neither
do they reap, nor gather into barns; yet your heavenly
Father feedeth them. Are ye not much better than
they?"
Matthew 6:26

Notes:

20

Tell It a-Goin'

Grandpa Holt was a man's man. Anyone could look to my grandpa, William K. Holt, and instantly recognize a work ethic that would carry him through his own life.

My first observance of his work ethic was in 1963 when the church that Dad pastored had to add rooms onto the church building. It was a volunteer work with various men of the church giving their time to the project. Grandpa heard of the building effort and the next day he came driving up in his GMC pickup.

Grandpa might not have had state of the art tools, but he knew his craft. The first thing he did was to look over the plans for the project and then at what was accomplished so far, and then he went to work. Men and materials were quickly organized and before long the addition to the church began to take shape. Days later the addition had the roof built and it was *dried in*. My grandpa knew what to do and how to do it.

Through the years I learned that Grandpa had done just about everything, including farming. He had a blacksmith shop on the farm and did his own welding in maintaining the equipment. He made syrup from the cane crop in his own syrup mill on the farm. In addition, he was an expert in building construction. In all his working, he was diligent and taught his children the importance of good work ethics.

It was natural for the kids working close together in picking cotton, or hoeing corn or cotton in season, to pass the time talking. Sometimes, however, the work slowed to a stop while they leaned on their hoes to talk. Grandpa would spot the inactivity and gently speak these familiar words: "Tell it a-Goin." That was then the work would again commence. Grandpa wasn't opposed to their conversation, it was the work stoppage that was unacceptable. So the solution was simple; talk while you work: 'Tell it a-Goin'.

The Bible has commentary on a work ethic in Proverbs chapter 14 verse 23,

"In all labour there is profit: but the talk of the lips tendeth only to penury."

Penury means very poor or extreme poverty. I don't know if my Grandpa Holt knew about this verse, but he knew the principle. If we are standing around talking then the work is not getting done. And if the work is not done we cannot collect our wages, and if we cannot collect wages then we can't provide a roof over our heads and food for the supper table.

I have worked with a lot of different people in my lifetime and some were not motivated to accomplish the assigned tasks. They would usually do no more than what's necessary to keep their position.

God addressed this issue in His word, the Bible. It says in Proverbs chapter 6 verse 6,

"Go to the ant, thou sluggard; consider her ways, and be wise."

Have you ever just watched an anthill? These wise little creatures of God's creation have a purpose and that is to serve their queen. They gather their food for winter and maintain or expand their nest as needed. I have never seen two ants standing still and talking! If they do talk, they 'Tell it a-Goin'.

Finally, the Bible gives us one more encouragement about doing our best when we work. In Colossians chapter 3 and verse 17,

"And whatsoever ye do in word or deed, do all in the name of the Lord Jesus, giving thanks to God and the Father by him."

So no matter if you are on the job or at home, do all as unto the Lord Jesus. If you mow the yard, or if you clean the house, do your best. If you are at work, do your best. And above all, keep working...'Tell it a-Goin'.

Additional Scriptures

"And whatsoever ye do, do it heartily, as to the Lord, and not unto men; 24 Knowing that of the Lord ye shall receive the reward of the inheritance: for ye serve the Lord Christ."
Colossians 3:23-24

"The soul of the sluggard desireth, and hath nothing: but the soul of the diligent shall be made fat."
Proverbs 13:4

"10 For even when we were with you, this we commanded you, that if any would not work, neither should he eat. 11 For we hear that there are some which walk among you disorderly, working not at all, but are busybodies. 12 Now them that are such we command and exhort by our Lord Jesus Christ, that with quietness they work, and eat their own bread."
II Thessalonians 3:10-13

"Commit thy works unto the LORD, and thy thoughts shall be established."
Proverbs 16:3

"Whether therefore ye eat, or drink, or whatsoever ye do, do all to the glory of God."
I Corinthians 10:31

"The husbandman that laboureth must be first partaker of the fruits."
II Timothy 2:6

Notes:

21

Enduring in Gain and Loss

I opened the statement for my retirement fund the other day and learned I will not be retiring anytime soon. The markets took a turn for the worse and so did my retirement. I guess I'd better keep my day job!

God is always aware of the situations in your life. He knows exactly who you are, where you are, and what's going on in your life. While we look at things considering the short term, God sees the future and all eternity. He knows the final outcome. In His infinite wisdom, He has worked all things out for our good and for His glory.

I've had my fair share of gain and loss. Admittedly it is easier to endure a gain rather than a loss, but both come from time to time into our lives. I have learned that whether I am blessed with gain or if I endure a loss, God is still on His throne in heaven.

Perhaps no one learned more about the greatness of God than a man named Job. He was a prosperous man that probably lived sometime after Noah's flood but before Moses. The devil claimed that Job honored God because of God's blessings in his life, therefore the LORD God allowed Job to be afflicted and he lost his wealth, his family, and even his health. It was a very difficult time for Job but he endured.

While Job was suffering, his friends came to comfort him and also tried to figure out why all this happened. There were moments when Job became discouraged and he eventually asked if he could talk directly to God about his troubles. In Job chapter 38 thru chapter 41 we have the narrative of this conversation between God and Job. Interestingly enough, Job didn't do much talking. Instead, God asked Job a series of questions, of which Job had no answers.

God asked Job where he was when God created the heavens and the earth. He then asked Job if he knew the dimensions of the earth. God asked Job if he could control the lightning or make it rain.

Could Job make the sun rise in the east, or could he control the journey of the stars across the sky? God asked Job if he could control a great beast many believe to be a dinosaur. God even asked Job if he could catch and tame a fire breathing dragon in Job chapter 41.

When God had concluded His questions, Job could do nothing but admit that God was supreme and in control of all things. Job continued to honor God with his life and eventually Job had more children and his wealth was restored. Job endured.

Perhaps that is the secret of enduring times of gain or loss; for no matter which comes into your life, God is in control.

And like Job, I cannot make the sun rise in the east, or make the winds blow or the rain to fall. I do not know the number of the stars in the sky nor can I control a wild beast, but I know that God can and will do all these things as He is sovereign of all.

It was Peter who wrote in First Peter chapter 4 and verse 19,

"Wherefore let them that suffer according to the will of God commit the keeping of their souls to him in well doing, as unto a faithful Creator."

The greatest comfort is trust in our Great and Faithful Creator. There is no one that loves us as He does. So the next time you are blessed with a gain or suffer a loss, turn to the Creator and trust in Him. You will endure.

Additional Scriptures

"For to me to live is Christ, and to die is gain."
Philippians 1:21

"By faith Moses, when he was come to years, refused to be called the son of Pharaoh's daughter; 25 Choosing rather to suffer affliction with the people of God, than to enjoy the pleasures of sin for a season; 26 Esteeming the reproach of Christ greater riches than the treasures in Egypt: for he had respect unto the recompence of the reward."
Hebrews 11:24-26

"But what things were gain to me, those I counted loss for Christ. 8 Yea doubtless, and I count all things but

loss for the excellency of the knowledge of Christ Jesus my Lord: for whom I have suffered the loss of all things, and do count them but dung, that I may win Christ, 9 And be found in him, not having mine own righteousness, which is of the law, but that which is through the faith of Christ, the righteousness which is of God by faith:"
Philippians 3:7-9

"Verily, verily, I say unto you, Except a corn of wheat fall into the ground and die, it abideth alone: but if it die, it bringeth forth much fruit. 25 He that loveth his life shall lose it; and he that hateth his life in this world shall keep it unto life eternal. 26 If any man serve me, let him follow me; and where I am, there shall also my servant be: if any man serve me, him will my Father honour."
John 12:24-26

"The young man saith unto him, All these things have I kept from my youth up: what lack I yet? 21 Jesus said unto him, If thou wilt be perfect, go and sell that thou hast, and give to the poor, and thou shalt have treasure in heaven: and come and follow me. 22 But when the young man heard that saying, he went away sorrowful: for he had great possessions."
Matthew 19:20-22

"And let the beauty of the LORD our God be upon us: and establish thou the work of our hands upon us; yea, the work of our hands establish thou it."
Psalm 90:17

Notes:

22

The Marriage Relationship Percentages

Many years ago I heard that a successful marriage is a 50-50 relationship. At the time it sounded good, after all 50 plus 50 equals 100, and I associated 100 as being the best it can be. Over the years I have heard the same formula from others. Now that my brain has more mileage on it I have reconsidered the math on a marriage relationship and desire to challenge these perceptions.

Jan and I have been married for nearly forty-two years. In 1974 we were young and very much in love. All we had was a 1964 Chevrolet Impala, two suitcases full of clothes, and the trunk of the Chevy was full of wedding presents. We didn't have any money, but I had a job.

Jan and I were not only young, we were very young. We didn't always make the right decisions but we did the best we could. Even as immature young people we were committed to each other to enjoy the success and to endure the failure of our choices. This brought us closer to each other as we began to mature. In effect, we grew up together.

I have heard the numbers tossed around and how the percentages of a marriage are rationalized. There was 60-40, and then 70-30, and an odd 80-20. Then the chores are rationalized...She does all the laundry while he does all the yard work. I believe these ideas are selfish and immature. To believe in these will only lead to heartache and failure.

You see, a successful marriage is 100-100. That's right, a 100 percent commitment of the man to the woman, and a 100 percent commitment of the woman to the man. A marriage is a lifetime adventure whose success is directly proportional to the commitment of the man and the woman to each other.

In this day and age where celebrities marry and divorce for the sake of getting their name in the news, it is refreshing to see married couples of all ages committed to each other, *"for better or worse, for richer or poorer, in sickness and in health, to cherish, love, and honor, 'til death do us part."*

With a percentage of 100-100 there is total commitment to the marriage. This means that anyone or anything other than your mate takes a secondary place in your life. Of course, we put the LORD God first.

When God performed the first wedding ceremony, the man Adam repeated this vow in Genesis chapter 2 and verse 24,

"Therefore shall a man leave his father and his mother, and shall cleave unto his wife: and they shall be one flesh."

The word *cleave* simply means to *'adhere', 'cling',* or *'stick fast.'* Looks like 100 percent!

The Biblical formula for a marriage is simple. The Apostle Paul wrote to the church in Ephesus the example for a marriage. In Ephesians chapter 5 and verse 22 and 25,

"Wives, submit yourselves unto your own husbands, as unto the Lord. 25 Husbands, love your wives, even as Christ also loved the church, and gave himself for it;"

The carnally minded might see these verses as outdated for the present day, but let's look again.

While the wife submits to her husband it does not mean that he is a dictator over her, but rather that she loves as well as respects him as her husband, as unto the Lord. Similarly, the husband is to love the wife as Christ loved the church, and gave himself for it.

The 100-100 percentage will build a stronger marriage, and that stronger marriage will build a stronger home. The only way to make the marriage even more secure is to make the Lord Jesus Christ the center of the home. I saw a wall plaque one time that said, "Christ is the head of this house, the unseen guest at every meal, the silent listener at every conversation."

Sounds like a winning formula to me.

Additional Scriptures

"A virtuous woman is a crown to her husband: but she that maketh ashamed is as rottenness in his bones."
Proverbs 12:4

"Whoso findeth a wife findeth a good thing, and obtaineth favour of the LORD."
Proverbs 18:22

"Live joyfully with the wife whom thou lovest all the days of the life of thy vanity, which he hath given thee under the sun, all the days of thy vanity: for that is thy portion in this life, and in thy labour which thou takest under the sun."
Ecclesiastes 9:9

"Be ye not unequally yoked together with unbelievers: for what fellowship hath righteousness with unrighteousness? and what communion hath light with darkness? 15 And what concord hath Christ with Belial? or what part hath he that believeth with an infidel?"
II Corinthians 6:14-15

"Marriage is honourable in all, and the bed undefiled: but whoremongers and adulterers God will judge."
Hebrews 13:4

"Likewise, ye wives, be in subjection to your own husbands; that, if any obey not the word, they also may without the word be won by the conversation of the wives;"
I Peter 3:1

Notes:

23

"LORD"... "Lord"... and ..."lord"

When the Bible was translated into English from the original Hebrew of the Old Testament and Greek of the New Testament they found different words that made reference to the Eternal and Self Sufficient God and the Lordship of Jesus Christ. Occasionally, the word "lord" is used to reference an individual in some sort of authority. To differentiate between the names of God and of an individual of authority we will find the words "LORD", "Lord", and "lord" in the Bible.

Unless a person notices the different use of capital and lower case letters and becomes curious as to their meaning then this revelation might not ever be known. I have found the distinctions to be a great blessing, so hang with me a couple of minutes and read on.

The word "LORD" is found many times in the Old Testament, beginning in Genesis chapter 2.

"These are the generations of the heavens and of the earth when they were created, in the day that the LORD God made the earth and the heavens."
Genesis 2:4

This spelling of LORD with all capital letters is taken from "Yahweh," the Hebrew name for God, which in short has been translated to "Jehovah."

Now we know from Exodus chapter 3 that "Yahweh" appeared to Moses out of the burning bush and revealed himself as "I AM THAT I AM".

"And Moses said unto God, Behold, when I come unto the children of Israel, and shall say unto them, The God of your fathers hath sent me unto you; and they shall say to me, What is his name? What shall I say unto them? 14 And God said unto Moses, I AM THAT I AM: and he said, Thus shalt thou say unto the children of Israel, I AM hath sent me unto you."
Exodus 3:13-14

Anytime that I see, "LORD" in the Old Testament I think of the Great I AM in Exodus chapter 3.

"Lord" is usually found in the New Testament in reference to the Lord Jesus Christ. Lord is taken from the Hebrew word "Adonai" which means "Master." Lord, therefore, is a title for Jesus denoting that He is the Master and supreme authority of all things. He is the Lord of our lives.

The word "lord" simply denotes a person in authority. In the book of Ruth chapter 2 and verse 13 a man by the name of Boaz has reapers harvesting his fields. Ruth joins the reapers and calls Boaz "my lord."

Something else I would like to share is the name for God. In Genesis chapter 1 and verse 1 it says,

*"In the beginning God created
the heaven and the earth".*

The translators of the English Bible found many different names for God but they simply translated them all to God. However, in Genesis Chapter 1 the name for God in the Hebrew text is, "Elohim" (El-o-heem) which means the "Strong Creator".

It excites me greatly when I read in the Bible names like "LORD God" which means "The Great I AM, The Strong Creator!" The same God that appeared to Moses out of the burning bush is the same LORD God that created all things!

The greatness of God is too high for us to comprehend. The Bible does give us perspective of understanding when it says in Deuteronomy,

"For the LORD your God is God of gods, and Lord of lords, a great God, a mighty, and a terrible, which regardeth not persons, nor taketh reward."
Deuteronomy 10:17

Notice the capital letters and lower case letters for God and Lord. *LORD* is the Great I AM, God is *Elohim*, *gods* is nothing, *Lord* is Master, and *lord* is human authority.

Perhaps all this is new to you and maybe confusing. Give it time, you will catch on. I only know that I am truly blessed by learning the distinctions of, "LORD, Lord, and lord".

May the LORD God (The Great I AM, The Strong Creator) bless you!

Additional Scriptures

"And one cried unto another, and said, Holy, holy, holy, is the LORD of hosts: the whole earth is full of his glory."
Isaiah 6:3

"And the four living creatures, each one of them having six wings, are full of eyes around and within; and day and night they do not cease to say, "HOLY, HOLY, HOLY is THE LORD GOD, THE ALMIGHTY, WHO WAS AND WHO IS AND WHO IS TO COME."
Revelation 4:8

"And, behold, there arose a great tempest in the sea, insomuch that the ship was covered with the waves: but he was asleep. 25 And his disciples came to him, and awoke him, saying, Lord, save us: we perish."
Matthew 8:24-25

"Ye call me Master and Lord: and ye say well; for so I am."
John 13:13

"And she said, Oh my lord, as thy soul liveth, my lord, I am the woman that stood by thee here, praying unto the LORD."

I Samuel 1:26

"Then the lords of the Philistines gathered them together for to offer a great sacrifice unto Dagon their god, and to rejoice: for they said, Our god hath delivered Samson our enemy into our hand."
Judges 16:23

Notes:

24

Specializing in the Impossible

One of the most loved and famous Christmas carols is "Silent Night." As we sing the first verse we visualize a cool, clear, and peaceful night filled with stars. Mother and child are wrapped against the chilled air as the child sleeps. The verse also mentions that Mary is a virgin.

How can it be that a virgin would give birth to a child? Our LORD God specializes in doing impossible things!

To the scientist it is impossible that God created the heaven and the earth in six days as it is written in Genesis chapter 1, but He did! God created the very vacuum of space itself, then created the earth. He made the light to shine on the earth and to fill the immense and infinite void of outer space. He made the atmosphere on the earth, then He formed the dry land. He created the plants in all their boundless varieties. He made the sun, the moon, then commanded all the stars to be created in their place. God even commanded the light of the stars to shine on the earth immediately and it was so...God broke the light barrier! God then made the innumerable varieties of aquatic life, birds, the animals, and man.

The Patriarch Abraham was promised that his descendants would be as the sand of the sea but Abraham had no son. Abraham was patient and trusting of God. When God visited with Abraham and Sarah and again promised that Abraham would have a son, Sarah laughed in her heart. You see, Sarah was very old and past the time of childbearing. God then asked a question, "Is anything too hard for the LORD?" About a year later, as promised, Sarah gave Abraham a son.

I take great joy in the fact that the Creator God, who made the heaven and the earth and all that in them is, has no problem making a woman who is past childbearing to have a son. The Creator God also has no problem allowing a virgin to bear a son. God specializes in doing the impossible.

The same Creator God of all things destroyed the world with a flood that covered the entire Earth while saving Noah and his family in an Ark of wood. He commanded the plagues that destroyed Egypt when He freed Israel from Egyptian bondage. He parted the waters of the Red Sea to allow Israel to flee the Egyptian armies. *"Impossible,"* you might say. Yeah, for man it is impossible. God specializes in the impossible.

It was the Lord Jesus Christ that walked on the water, made the blind to see, the deaf to hear, the mute to speak, He healed the sick, cleansed the leprous man, and put a wild man in his right mind. Jesus turned the water into wine, fed five thousand men with five small biscuits and a couple pieces of fish, and calmed the storm, and Jesus even raised Lazarus from the grave after he had been dead four days! Impossible for man, but not for God.

The Creator God, who specializes in doing the impossible, can take all your cares and burdens if you will give them to Him. He is interested in all aspects of your life, no matter how big or how insignificant you think it might be. It was Jesus that said in Matthew chapter 11 verse 28,

"Come unto me, all you that labour and are heavy laden, and I will give you rest."

You have to admit that this is a great offer. Your burdens and problems are not impossible for God. Only the true and living God can do these things.

Make this a time to remember by placing your trust in the LORD. He specializes in the impossible!

Additional Scriptures

"For with God nothing shall be impossible."
Luke 1:37

"But Jesus beheld them, and said unto them, With men this is impossible; but with God all things are possible."
Matthew 19:26

"Is any thing too hard for the LORD? At the time appointed I will return unto thee, according to the time of life, and Sarah shall have a son."
Genesis 18:14

"Ah LORD God! behold, thou hast made the heaven and the earth by thy great power and stretched out arm, and there is nothing too hard for thee:"
Jeremiah 32:17

"Behold, I am the LORD, the God of all flesh: is there any thing too hard for me?"
Jeremiah 32:27

"Fear thou not; for I am with thee: be not dismayed; for I am thy God: I will strengthen thee; yea, I will help thee; yea, I will uphold thee with the right hand of my righteousness."
Isaiah 41:10

Notes:

25

Mrs. Richardson's Carrot Cake

I have learned in my life that there are certain words that simply don't belong together. For example, egg and plant, efficient and government, honest and politician. When I was around 9 years old I heard two words that I instinctively knew didn't belong together; carrot and cake.

In 1963 there was an older couple that lived very close to us and attended Dad's church. Raymond Richardson and his wife Leona were great people. They not only attended Dad's church but they were very active. Brother Raymond would attend to ushering duties and Leona would play the church organ. She could also sing...about an octave above everyone else!

Since they lived close to the church we were invited occasionally to their house for a visit. Leona was a great hostess and cook. One time while we were there she offered me a piece of her carrot cake. Instantly in my mind I knew something was fundamentally wrong. How could it be that someone would use the word *carrot* and the word *cake* in the same sentence? I politely declined the offer for the cake.

Meanwhile, my parents were enjoying their serving of the cake. I guess that Mrs. Leona could see the amazement in my eyes as I watched my parents enjoy each bite of their cake so she gave me a second chance. Once again, she offered me a piece of carrot cake. This time I accepted.

As I put the first bite in my mouth I was totally unprepared for the ecstasy of flavor that ensued. The cake was light and moist, the icing was sweet and very pleasant. I was hooked. It wasn't long that I was asking for a second piece of cake. Mrs. Richardson enthusiastically obliged.

The Bible says in Psalm 34 verse 8,

> *"O taste and see that the LORD is good:*
> *blessed is the man that trusteth in him."*

Just like my aversion to the idea of carrot cake, many folks are simply not willing to taste and see that the LORD is good. Perhaps the words *blessed* and *trust* just don't seem to go together. Let's briefly examine these words.

The word *trust* is defined as, *"a firm belief in the reliability, truth, ability, or strength of someone or something."*

People place a measure of trust in their bank, otherwise they would not keep their money in that bank. Another example is the trust we place in our employer for a steady paycheck. If there was a chance we would not be paid, we would likely seek other employment.

Trusting in God is very similar to the aforementioned examples. We are encouraged to trust in the LORD God again and again in the Scriptures. It means that we anchor our lives in God.

It is an attitude of our soul and mind of our need and for the sufficiency of God wherein we can rest.

The second word in that verse is *blessed*. The definition of blessed is, *"bringing pleasure, contentment, or good fortune."* Some people associate being blessed with being materially prosperous. We must remember that the blessings of God are spiritual, heavenly, and eternal, and as a rule not earthly prosperity.

By trusting in God we have a peace in our heart that the world cannot understand. It was the Psalmist that wrote of trusting in God in Psalm 1 and verse 3,

"And he shall be like a tree planted by the rivers of water, that bringeth forth his fruit in his season; his leaf also shall not wither; and whatsoever he doeth shall prosper."

Mrs. Richardson's carrot cake was very good, but it was temporal and only lasted a few minutes. Trusting in God is blessed and eternal; and eternal is a long, long time.

Additional Scriptures

"The God of my rock; in him will I trust: he is my shield, and the horn of my salvation, my high tower, and my refuge, my saviour; thou savest me from violence."
II Samuel 22:3

"As for God, his way is perfect; the word of the LORD is tried: he is a buckler to all them that trust in him."
II Samuel 22:31

"Some trust in chariots, and some in horses: but we will remember the name of the LORD our God."
Psalm 20:7

"Judge me, O LORD; for I have walked in mine integrity: I have trusted also in the LORD; therefore I shall not slide."
Psalm 26:1

"In whom ye also trusted, after that ye heard the word of truth, the gospel of your salvation: in whom also after that ye believed, ye were sealed with that holy Spirit of promise,"
Ephesians 1:13

"The LORD is good, a strong hold in the day of trouble; and he knoweth them that trust in him."
Nahum 1:7

Notes:

26

The Art of Being a Squeaky Wheel

We've all done it...we ask our parents for something and they said, *"NO."* Undaunted by their answer, we go back again, and again they say, *"NO."* With grim determination, we go back and ask once again, and the more they say, *"NO,"* the more we go back. Finally, the answer is, *"Yes."*

Perhaps they say *yes* just to get us out of their hair, or maybe they say *no* just to see how far we would push the issue, but at the end of the day they say, *"Yes."* The squeaky wheel gets the grease!

Prayer is a powerful tool in the life of a Christian, however, we pray far too little. For most folks, their prayer is at the dinner table. I believe that God is grieved that we spend so little time with Him in prayer. Some people doubt that God will hear, much less answer their prayers.

On the other hand, the devil is happy with that. He likes it because he knows that the power of God in your life becomes anemic with the lack of prayer. You are the weakest when you are spiritually anemic, but the devil will deceive you into believing that you are a tower of spiritual strength. Solomon gave insight here in Proverbs chapter 25,

"Whoso boasteth himself of a false gift is like clouds and wind without rain."
Proverbs 25:14

The devil has deceived us into believing we don't need to spend time with our Heavenly Father by reading the Bible or communing in prayer.

Christian people need to be burdened to the point where only time in prayer and in the Word of God will satisfy their souls. In effect, when it comes to prayer, the best prayer to the Father will be like a squeaky wheel!

What I am about to say might surprise you, but it is OK to bother God! In the book of Isaiah chapter 62 and verses 6-7 it says,

"I have set watchmen upon thy walls, O Jerusalem, which shall never hold their peace day nor night: ye that make mention of the LORD, keep not silence, And give him no rest, till he establish, and till he make Jerusalem a praise in the earth."

The first sign you are a squeaky wheel in prayer is that you are a watchman, meaning simply that you are ever ready when an opportunity arises to go to the Father and pray.

Another sign you are a squeaky wheel in prayer is that you will not give God any rest. We must continually be taking our request to Him! Finally, you don't give up until you hear from Him,

"And give Him no rest, until He establishes."
Isaiah 62:7

No wonder the Apostle Paul wrote in First Thessalonians chapter 5 and verse 17,

"Pray without ceasing."

Appears to me the Apostle wanted us to be squeaky wheels, always going again and again to the Heavenly Father in prayer.

We honor the LORD God when we take Him our petitions in prayer. Because God is omniscient (or all knowing) He already knows what is in your life, He knows your burdens, and He even knows what you will pray before you pray it. The secret is that God wants us to know the burdens of life and demonstrate to Him that we trust Him to take care of them.

Be a squeaky wheel, and trust in Him!

Additional Scriptures

"Therefore I say unto you, What things soever ye desire, when ye pray, believe that ye receive them, and ye shall have them."
Mark 11:24

"Ask, and it shall be given you; seek, and ye shall find; knock, and it shall be opened unto you: 8 For every one that asketh receiveth; and he that seeketh findeth; and to him that knocketh it shall be opened."
Matthew 7:7-8

"And all things, whatsoever ye shall ask in prayer, believing, ye shall receive."
Matthew 21:22

"Be careful for nothing; but in every thing by prayer and supplication with thanksgiving let your requests be made known unto God. 7 And the peace of God, which passeth all understanding, shall keep your hearts and minds through Christ Jesus."
Philippians 4:6-7

"Pray without ceasing"
I Thessalonians 5:17

"Evening, and morning, and at noon, will I pray, and cry aloud: and he shall hear my voice."
Psalm 55:17

Notes:

27

The Earth Moved

When I was a child my mother would read a Bible chapter to me at bedtime. I developed a yearning for my favorite chapters...which are Genesis chapter 1 and Psalm 24. Little did I know at the time the influence these scriptures would have on my life.

Genesis chapter 1 is the creation narrative which says that God made the heavens and the earth and everything in them. It is by faith we as Christians believe the account in Genesis chapter one.

"Through faith we understand that the worlds were framed by the word of God."
Hebrews 11:3

God not only created the heavens and the earth, but He owns the earth and all the people in it!

"The earth is the LORD's, and the fulness thereof; the world, and they that dwell therein."
Psalm 24:1

According to the Bible both you and I belong to God!

The earth and man were both created in Divine perfection, but it did not remain perfect very long. Most everyone has heard of Adam and Eve in the Garden of Eden and how they ate the forbidden fruit. It was a defining moment in history because man chose to replace obedience to God with his own self will. Man sinned and forever impacted the relationship between God and man.

As a result of sin, God said that the serpent would crawl on its belly, the woman would give birth in sorrow, and for Adam the ground was cursed. It would no longer be easy to harvest food from the earth.

The Bible says that the earth begin to grow thorns and thistles. Have you ever gotten a sticker or a sand burr in your foot? You can thank Adam for that. Have you ever tried to get all the weeds out of your vegetable garden or flower beds? You can thank Adam for that. The earth moved from being predictable in planting and harvesting to unpredictable and difficult, thus frustrating those that work the ground. The ground is cursed because of sin.

I recently saw all the cracks in the ground around our house and realized the cracks are there because the ground is cursed. Most folks would say it's because of the lack of rain, but remember that God cursed the ground.

Ever wondered why the foundation of your house is constantly moving and shifting? Doors do not close properly and cracks develop in the walls. The ground is cursed.

Have you ever wondered why a new highway will develop waves in the pavement after a few months? It's because the ground under the highway is cursed.

In all things we are to honor and praise our Creator God. For when we praise our God, the other things like cracks in the foundation or weeds in the garden or other difficulties of life shouldn't bother us. That great old hymn says:

"Turn your eyes upon Jesus,
Look full in His wonderful face.
And the things of earth will grow strangely dim,
In the light of His glory and grace."

The ground may be cursed, but God still loves us immensely. You belong to Him, and He desires to be your friend. Make room in your heart today for The LORD God.

Additional Scriptures

"In the beginning God created the heaven and the earth."
Genesis 1:1

"And unto Adam he said, Because thou hast hearkened unto the voice of thy wife, and hast eaten of the tree, of which I commanded thee, saying, Thou shalt not eat of it: cursed is the ground for thy sake; in sorrow shalt thou eat of it all the days of thy life; 18 Thorns also and thistles shall it bring forth to thee; and thou shalt eat the herb of the field; 19 In the sweat of thy face shalt thou eat

bread, till thou return unto the ground; for out of it wast thou taken: for dust thou art, and unto dust shalt thou return."
Genesis 3:17-19

"But God, who is rich in mercy, for his great love wherewith he loved us, 5 Even when we were dead in sins, hath quickened us together with Christ, (by grace ye are saved;) 6 And hath raised us up together, and made us sit together in heavenly places in Christ Jesus: 7 That in the ages to come he might shew the exceeding riches of his grace in his kindness toward us through Christ Jesus."
Ephesians 2:4-7

"But God commendeth his love toward us, in that, while we were yet sinners, Christ died for us."
Romans 5:8

"God setteth the solitary in families: he bringeth out those which are bound with chains: but the rebellious dwell in a dry land."
Psalm 68:6

"Looking unto Jesus the author and finisher of our faith; who for the joy that was set before him endured the cross, despising the shame, and is set down at the right hand of the throne of God."
Hebrews 12:2

Notes:

28

Gazing at the Glory of God

One of my favorite pastimes is gazing at the stars on a clear and cool winter evening. If you catch a moonless night for stargazing the view of the sky is absolutely stunning.

I believe there is something special about taking the time to gaze at the stars. For me, it is a vivid reminder of the fourth day of Creation when the LORD God created the sun, the moon, and the stars. The Bible tells us in Psalm 33 and verse 6,

"By the word of the LORD were the heavens made; and all the host of them by the breath of his mouth."

God literally spoke the stars into existence!

As I gaze towards the night sky I can only identify a couple of constellations...mostly Orion, the Big Dipper, and the Little Dipper. I can also find the North Star, Polaris. After I identify those heavenly bodies I sit still and watch the sky while being refreshed by the chill of the night air. I then begin to see the *depth* of God's creative handiwork in the night sky.

Those marvelous points of light in the night sky were created by God himself. He had no help; He needed no help. He simply commanded by the word of His mouth and the stars were formed by His will and for His glory. As we look into the night sky we see flickering lights, but the reality is these stars are thousands of light years apart and most of these stars are quite huge compared to our own sun.

Another remarkable fact is that the stars are actually very simple in their composition. They are about 73 percent hydrogen and 25 percent helium. The remaining 2 percent is a mix of other elements. Essentially, stars are huge balls of gas with nuclear fusion reactions inside them that give off light and heat. And there is more: when God created the stars He commanded them to shine their light on the earth and immediately it was done. God broke the light barrier so that stars at such great distances away from the earth could be seen immediately.

The Bible also says that God knows the number of the stars and He knows them all by name.

"Lift up your eyes on high, and behold who hath created these things, that bringeth out their host by number: he calleth them all by names by the greatness of his might, for that he is strong in power; not one faileth."
Isaiah 40:26

As I gaze into the depths of the night sky I recall one of my favorite verses in the Bible: Psalm 19 and verse 1,

"The heavens declare the glory of God; and the firmament sheweth his handywork."

The night sky is certainly beautiful. From a human point of view we can gaze into the incomprehensible infinity and immensity of God. Sometimes as I look at the stars I wonder what God named the star I'm looking at.

At the next clear and cool evening we have why not take the opportunity to gaze into the night sky. Take the time to focus on God's incredible handiwork and a portion of His stunning glory. Peace is gazing at the stars with the knowledge that you know their Creator.

One more thing, leave your cell phone in the house! No distractions allowed.

Additional Scriptures

"When I consider thy heavens, the work of thy fingers, the moon and the stars, which thou hast ordained; 4 What is man, that thou art mindful of him? and the son of man, that thou visitest him?"
Psalm 8:3-4

"Seek him that maketh the seven stars and Orion, and turneth the shadow of death into the morning, and maketh the day dark with night: that calleth for the waters of the sea, and poureth them out upon the face of the earth: The LORD is his name:"
Amos 5:8

"And lest thou lift up thine eyes unto heaven, and when thou seest the sun, and the moon, and the stars, even all the host of heaven, shouldest be driven to worship them, and serve them, which the LORD thy God hath divided unto all nations under the whole heaven."
Deuteronomy 4:19

"And let them be for lights in the firmament of the heaven to give light upon the earth: and it was so. 16 And God made two great lights; the greater light to rule the day, and the lesser light to rule the night: he made the stars also."
Genesis 1:15-16

"Thou, even thou, art LORD alone; thou hast made heaven, the heaven of heavens, with all their host, the earth, and all things that are therein, the seas, and all that is therein, and thou preservest them all; and the host of heaven worshippeth thee."
Nehemiah 9:6

"He healeth the broken in heart, and bindeth up their wounds. 4 He telleth the number of the stars; he calleth them all by their names. 5 Great is our LORD, and of great power: his understanding is infinite."
Psalm 147:3-5

Notes:

29

The Insolence of Dirty Shoes

Have you ever walked inside the house wearing your dirty shoes? If you got caught you probably had to deal with the consequences. It recently happened to me.

I was in the yard mowing when my little lawn tractor got stuck in a soft spot of ground. With the help of a short piece of rope tied to the tractor I pulled it out of the soft spot. Since it was nearly dark I decided to call it a day on the mowing. I parked the lawn tractor in the shed and went into the house. After wiping off my shoes I thought it was safe to go inside the house, but I tracked mud from the back door to the bedroom. It really wasn't that much mud, but still enough to get me into trouble with my wife of 41 years! Obviously she has a higher standard for me to hold to.

I am reminded of the encounter between God and Moses in Exodus chapter 3. Moses was keeping the sheep of his father-in-law when he saw a bush burning yet the bush was not consumed. Moses decided to take a closer look. As he approached the burning bush, God called out to him from the bush and Moses answered. The first thing God told him to do is to take off his shoes because the place where he was standing was holy ground.

In many ways we have lost our concept of the holiness of God. The Bible gives us glimpses of worship in the presence of the LORD yet we ignore these for the most part. It was A. W. Tozer that said that no people will ever rise above their religion. I have taken that a step further in that no church will ever rise higher than its concept of God.

Pulling off the shoes is an emblem of laying aside the pollutions contracted by walking in the world and in the way of sin. God is Holy. As we come into His presence it is insolence for us to approach Him with *dirty shoes*. I speak not of the literal shoes on your feet, but the spiritual shoes of your heart.

Insolence is one of those 10 dollar words that means, *"Rude and disrespectful behavior."* God had Moses to remove his shoes before approaching the burning bush because He was teaching Moses that we must leave behind our walk in the world when we approach God.

It is very important that when we read the Word of God that we abandon our walk in this world as we allow the Living Word to enrich our being. When we pray, we should come to God giving Him praise and glory. When we worship, we must approach God in the spirit, leaving behind the trappings of this world to worship Him in the Spirit. Remember that we live in a wicked world and it is insolence when we do not approach the Living God on His terms.

I guess I am old fashioned in that I believe we should attend church regularly and that we go with our hearts prepared to sing praises to God and to learn from the preaching of God's Word. We should dress appropriately and behave respectfully. After all, worship is all about our LORD God, the Creator of all things.

Finally, the Bible says in Ephesians 5 and verse 15 and 16,

"See then that ye walk circumspectly, not as fools, but as wise, Redeeming the time, because the days are evil."

To walk circumspectly means to, *"think carefully about possible risks before doing or saying something."* That should help to keep your shoes clean!

Additional Scriptures

"And he said, Draw not nigh hither: put off thy shoes from off thy feet, for the place whereon thou standest is holy ground."
Exodus 3:5

"And the captain of the LORD's host said unto Joshua, Loose thy shoe from off thy foot; for the place whereon thou standest is holy. And Joshua did so."
Joshua 5:15

"Let us therefore come boldly unto the throne of grace, that we may obtain mercy, and find grace to help in time of need."

Hebrews 4:16

"Draw nigh to God, and he will draw nigh to you. Cleanse your hands, ye sinners; and purify your hearts, ye double minded."
James 4:8

"And ye shall seek me, and find me, when ye shall search for me with all your heart."
Jeremiah 29:13

"Blessed are the pure in heart: for they shall see God."
Matthew 5:8

Notes:

30

Love Letters Straight from the Heart

Jan and I met at Baptist Bible College in Springfield, Missouri. In 1972 we were both freshmen, but we only had one class together; an afternoon English class at 1:00 PM. Mrs. Johnson, our professor, was nice enough, but still old fashioned in that she wanted the entire class in alphabetical order. The front row was A-G and the second row was H thru something, I don't remember. I do know that Jan Callaway sat in front of Louis Holmes.

At the time, Jan's long reddish hair and those luscious big curls so common in 1972 were all over my desk. Unable to resist the temptation, I rolled those long curls in the palm of my hand and flipped them to the air with ecstasy. Jan would run back to the dorm at lunch time and re-roll her hair just so I would play in it. The plan worked.

My first semester of school I was way overloaded with class and work. I took the second semester off just to rest. At the Easter break I went back to Springfield to visit friends. I found Jan and she gave me her mailbox number at the college. Having the mailbox number of a girl at Bible College was like owning a gold mine. Box 512. When I returned home we began to write.

This generation is much different with texting, Twitter, Facebook, and the like. In 1972 we had two options, write letters and wait several days for a reply, or save LOTS of money for a long distance call. Our communication was taken care of by Uncle Sam and Ma Bell.

Through the medium of letters we grew to know each other and eventually fell in love. Sometimes we would write to each other without a reply first. When the heart yearns with love, sometimes what you have to say can't wait for the next reply.

I have often heard that the Bible is God's love letter to man. It explains just what we need to know about all things, including God's love for man. God wants us to know the benefits of obeying His commandments and His law. God also wants us to know the consequences of disobedience. It can get ugly at times, but it is a truth we need to know.

The Bible opens with the narrative of Creation in Genesis chapter one. A person might ask how the Creation account would show God's love to me. It is simple. God, in his omnipotent wisdom, knew that man would concoct the theory of the big bang, the age of the universe, how the earth was made, and the nature of the universe. However, the longest conversation between man and God recorded in Scripture is in Job chapter 38 thru 41. God assured Job that in all of his problems that God was the Creator and that the Creator is in control. Job could not control the weather, Job could not give the dimensions of the earth, Job could not control the animals including a dinosaur or a fire breathing dragon. But God can. And we, like Job, can take great comfort in God's love for us that He is in control of everything in our lives.

Peter also wrote in First Peter chapter 4 and verse 19,

"Wherefore let them that suffer according to the will of God commit the keeping of their souls to him in well doing, as unto a faithful Creator."

We can know that God loves us because He is faithful, and all powerful, and in control of all things. While we might be suffering on this earth we can trust our Creator God to keep our souls.

So read God's love letter to man. You probably have a love letter waiting for you under the coffee table, or perhaps on your night stand, or on top of the refrigerator. It is long overdue.

Additional Scriptures

"O LORD, thou hast searched me, and known me. 2 Thou knowest my downsitting and mine uprising, thou understandest my thought afar off. 3 Thou compassest my path and my lying down, and art acquainted with all my ways. 4 For there is not a word in my tongue, but, lo, O LORD, thou knowest it altogether. 5 Thou hast beset me behind and before, and laid thine hand upon me. 6 Such knowledge is too wonderful for me; it is high, I cannot attain unto it."

Psalm 139:1-6

"Are not two sparrows sold for a farthing? and one of them shall not fall on the ground without your Father. 30 But the very hairs of your head are all numbered. 31 Fear ye not therefore, ye are of more value than many sparrows."
Matthew 10:29-31

"Before I formed thee in the belly I knew thee; and before thou camest forth out of the womb I sanctified thee, and I ordained thee a prophet unto the nations."
Jeremiah 1:5

"This I recall to my mind, therefore have I hope. 22 It is of the LORD's mercies that we are not consumed, because his compassions fail not. 23 They are new every morning: great is thy faithfulness."
Lamentations 3:21-23

"Beloved, let us love one another: for love is of God; and every one that loveth is born of God, and knoweth God. 8 He that loveth not knoweth not God; for God is love. 9 In this was manifested the love of God toward us, because that God sent his only begotten Son into the world, that we might live through him. 10 Herein is love, not that we loved God, but that he loved us, and sent his Son to be the propitiation for our sins. 11 Beloved, if God so loved

*us, we ought also to love one another. 12 No man
hath seen God at any time.
If we love one another, God dwelleth in us,
and his love is perfected in us."*
I John 4:7-12

*"For God so loved the world, that he gave his only
begotten Son, that whosoever believeth in him
should not perish, but have everlasting life."*
John 3:16

Notes:

31

Love Letters – Part 2

Just as Jan and I fell in love while writing letters to each other, my Mom and Dad wrote letters to each other in the late 1940's.

When my Dad was just seventeen he joined the Army. My grandmother, Virginia Holmes, had to sign the papers so that Dad could enlist. When Dad joined he met Charles Holt. In time, Charles noticed that Dad did not get any mail and suggested that he write to his cousin, Edna Holt, in Texas.

There was the first letter, then the second. They began writing letters back and forth to each other. Back then, they had no cell phones, no Twitter, no Facebook, or even email. Snail mail was the only way to communicate at the time. Letters took a long time since they had to cross the Pacific Ocean, but they wrote.

Early in Dad's military career he was sent to Japan. At the time Japan was occupied by the United States after World War Two. When the Korean War broke out, my Dad was sent to Korea.

The letters, drawings, and pictures went back and forth half way around the world. Back then, I was just a twinkle in Dad's eye. Things were beginning to happen as my future Mom and Dad carefully wrote what was on their hearts in each letter.

The letters were like gold for a young man far from home in Korea and for a farm girl in Texas. Each word written on the page was very precious. The letters were read, then read again. With great excitement, answers were prepared to be sent back. Hearts were opened and would cling to each and every word.

The Bible says in Proverbs 25 and verse 11,

*"A word fitly spoken is like
apples of gold in pictures of silver."*

I am sure that whether the word is spoken or written, it is still like gold. God has expressed His love for us in His Word, the Bible. The most famous of these is John 3 and verse 16,

"For God so loved the world, that he gave his only begotten Son, that whosoever believeth in him should not perish, but have everlasting life."

Further, in First John chapter 3 and verse 1,

"Behold, what manner of love the Father hath bestowed upon us, that we should be called the sons of God:"

All these wonderful verses are in the Bible that you have in your home. Go and find your Bible and search these verses yourself. Mark them, meditate on them, and thank God for loving you.

The Bible truly is God's love letter to man. He is telling us in His word that He loves you so much that He wants you to accept Jesus Christ and cleanse you from all your sin. God is holy, and the only way to Him is through Jesus Christ. That is why Jesus died on the cross, so that when we have salvation through Jesus Christ that God does not see our sin, He sees Jesus.

When Dad's duty was done in Korea, he was sent back to the States to finish his time in the Army. Dad and my Grandmother Holmes rode a bus from Benton, Illinois to Oklaunion, Texas so Dad could meet this charming girl he had that was more than a pen pal. Back in those days there were no Interstate Highways, so a bus trip took a while.

Mom and Dad met for the first time on Tuesday, June 5, 1951, and were married a few days later on a Sunday, June 10, 1951. They are approaching 65 years together. And to think it all started as a suggestion from a stranger.

Additional Scriptures

"Behold, what manner of love the Father hath bestowed upon us, that we should be called the sons of God: therefore the world knoweth us not, because it knew him not."
I John 3:1

"These things have I written unto you that believe on the name of the Son of God; that ye may know that ye have eternal life, and that ye may believe on the name

of the Son of God. 14 And this is the confidence that we have in him, that, if we ask any thing according to his will, he heareth us:"
I John 5:13-14

"Let not your heart be troubled: ye believe in God, believe also in me. 2 In my Father's house are many mansions: if it were not so, I would have told you. I go to prepare a place for you. 3 And if I go and prepare a place for you, I will come again, and receive you unto myself; that where I am, there ye may be also."
John 14:1-3

"Be strong and of a good courage, fear not, nor be afraid of them: for the LORD thy God, he it is that doth go with thee; he will not fail thee, nor forsake thee."
Deuteronomy 31:6

"For I am persuaded, that neither death, nor life, nor angels, nor principalities, nor powers, nor things present, nor things to come, 39 Nor height, nor depth, nor any other creature, shall be able to separate us from the love of God, which is in Christ Jesus our Lord."
Romans 8:38-39

"Casting all your care upon him; for he careth for you."
I Peter 5:7

Notes:

32

When Pain is Preferred

I went to the dentist for my checkup and the hygienist asked if I was having any issues. I promptly confessed that I had a tooth that had hurt for a few days but now it was OK. As I was hoping for another reprieve the hygienist took some x-rays in the suspicious area and promptly called the doctor. I knew it would not be good.

The good doctor did an exam then asked me to go to a specialist for another look at this tooth. Grudgingly I went. I really thought everything was OK. After all I had no pain and all seemed normal. Besides, I had other places I would rather spend the consulting fees.

The specialist was kind enough. We looked at x-rays of my teeth like we were looking through an old family picture album. He then looked at this offending tooth. I was surprised when he asked to check sensitivity. He took a piece of frozen cotton and gently touched all the teeth around the tooth that was the star of this rodeo. All those teeth really hurt when touched with the frozen cotton. He said that was a good sign. I was relieved. He then touched the frozen cotton to the main attraction, the tooth, the star of the show. I felt no pain.

To my disappointment that tooth was pronounced dead or near death. It was time to open my wallet and my mouth for additional dental work.

Had that tooth been sensitive to the pain, the outcome would have likely been much different.

Our bodies feel pain as a signal that something is wrong or needs attention. Our minds can also feel pain, grief, and remorse as we work through various experiences in our lives. The key point here is when we feel pain in our hearts it means we are sensitive and empathetic to others. The pain is a sign of life.

The Apostle Paul wrote these words about insensitive people.

"Now the Spirit speaketh expressly, that in the latter times some shall depart from the faith, giving heed to seducing spirits, and doctrines of devils; 2 Speaking lies in hypocrisy; having their conscience seared with a hot iron;"
I Timothy 4:1

A conscience seared with a hot iron will no longer feel pain like calloused hands no longer feel the discomfort of work.

By being sensitive and feeling pain in our hearts and minds we are vulnerable, but we are also better able to respond to those who are experiencing pain in their lives.

God too feels our pain and sorrow. He desires to wrap his strong arms of love around us and hold us tight to His bosom for He knows exactly what we are experiencing.

We know that our Heavenly Father knows exactly where you are and what you are enduring. You see, if He was not empathetic to events in our lives He would be a God that didn't care. But He does care, immensely. The Bible tells us that The LORD God will bind up the wounds of the brokenhearted. He knows you are enduring pain in your heart and that you desire relief.

No one likes to experience pain, but hopefully we can appreciate the benefits from it. God does. For the Lord Jesus Christ experienced horrific pain as He died on the cross. He shed His blood and died for us for the punishment of sin. Therefore, because of His death and resurrection, Jesus Christ is our advocate.

When we all stand before God, the believer has his sins covered because of the death and resurrection of Jesus Christ. The unbeliever will not. Yes, pain was involved, but the debt of sin is paid. Thank you LORD for saving my soul, thank you LORD for making me whole, thank you LORD for giving to me, thy salvation so rich and free.

Additional Scriptures

"The LORD is nigh unto them that are of a broken heart; and saveth such as be of a contrite spirit."
Psalm 34:18

"For in that he himself hath suffered being tempted, he is able to succour them that are tempted."

Hebrews 2:18

"There hath no temptation taken you but such as is common to man: but God is faithful, who will not suffer you to be tempted above that ye are able; but will with the temptation also make a way to escape, that ye may be able to bear it."
I Corinthians 10:13

"Be sober, be vigilant; because your adversary the devil, as a roaring lion, walketh about, seeking whom he may devour: 9 Whom resist stedfast in the faith, knowing that the same afflictions are accomplished in your brethren that are in the world. 10 But the God of all grace, who hath called us unto his eternal glory by Christ Jesus, after that ye have suffered a while, make you perfect, stablish, strengthen, settle you. 11 To him be glory and dominion for ever and ever. Amen."
I Peter 5:8-11

"For thus saith the high and lofty One that inhabiteth eternity, whose name is Holy; I dwell in the high and holy place, with him also that is of a contrite and humble spirit, to revive the spirit of the humble, and to revive the heart of the contrite ones."
Isaiah 57:15

"He healeth the broken in heart, and bindeth up their wounds."
Psalm 147:3

Notes:

33

What Did He Say?

I was enjoying a leisurely lunch in a restaurant when these two distinguished gentlemen came in and sat at the next table. I was eating and pondering my next sermon when these guys started a conversation in their native tongue. I do not know the language but it seemed that every syllable blazed its way at lightning speed.

A little known biblical fact is that at one time the whole earth was of one language. Actually, the whole world was of one language for about 1800 years after Creation.

Man was thrown out of the Garden of Eden after he sinned, and his sin was grievous to God. But everyone spoke the same language. I do not know what the language was, nor does the Bible say, but we do know that the language was given to man by God. Imagine, being able to speak the original God given language. Since it was a God given language, I would postulate that one's meaning would be perfectly clear when spoken. I guess we will find out in heaven. Perhaps when we get to heaven we will speak that language once again

When God told Noah to build the ark around 1400 years after Creation, everyone still spoke the same language. It took Noah 120 years to build the ark, and everyone listening, watching, or laughing heard of impending judgement by God. The LORD

God is so patient, allowing plenty of time for people to decide to follow Him.

After the flood, people still spoke the same language. Noah, Noah's wife, Noah's three sons, and their wives spoke the same language. As sons and daughters were born, they were taught the same language, and so on, and so on.

So where did all the different languages come from?

Man is carnal, and therefore disobedient to God. Man was told by God to scatter and populate the earth. In their disobedience they stayed together, and when they came to the Plain of Shinar, (probably in modern Iraq), they decided to build a tower and a city that would reach unto heaven. This displeased God because this city and this tower were of false religions that do not recognize the Creator as God. Many believe this is the origins of what we call modern astrology.

God, in an instant of time, confounded the language so that they would not understand each other. So, some spoke what became German, some spoke what became Spanish. Some spoke a different dialect yet. Long story short, men working on the tower no longer understood each other. Work on the tower and the false religions stopped.

Afterward, men and women that spoke the same language would form families and tribes that scattered all over the earth. Stronger groups would persecute weaker groups, and the scattering continued.

Language is constantly changing. For example, when the King James Bible was first published after 1611, the language was perfectly normal to the men and women of the time. I have seen a reprint of the original King James and it is a very difficult read, however, the King James Bible we have today is more up-to-date English. One can even purchase versions of the Bible that are even more colloquial for these times.

No matter what your language, the message from God is still the same. He loves us with an incredible, incomprehensible love, He has provided a pardon for our sins, and He desires for all of us to live in heaven eternally with Him. The only words that must be spoken are the words where you acknowledge Jesus Christ as Savior. And God understands every language perfectly.

Additional Scriptures

"And they said one to another, Go to, let us make brick, and burn them thoroughly. And they had brick for stone, and slime had they for morter. 4 And they said, Go to, let us build us a city and a tower, whose top may reach unto heaven; and let us make us a name, lest we be scattered abroad upon the face of the whole earth."
Genesis 11:3-4

"Go to, let us go down, and there confound their language, that they may not understand one

another's speech. 8 So the LORD scattered them abroad from thence upon the face of all the earth: and they left off to build the city. 9 Therefore is the name of it called Babel; because the LORD did there confound the language of all the earth: and from thence did the LORD scatter them abroad upon the face of all the earth."
Genesis 11:7-9

"After this I beheld, and, lo, a great multitude, which no man could number, of all nations, and kindreds, and people, and tongues, stood before the throne, and before the Lamb, clothed with white robes, and palms in their hands; 10 And cried with a loud voice, saying, Salvation to our God which sitteth upon the throne, and unto the Lamb."
Revelation 7:9-10

"And hath made of one blood all nations of men for to dwell on all the face of the earth, and hath determined the times before appointed, and the bounds of their habitation; 27 That they should seek the Lord, if haply they might feel after him, and find him, though he be not far from every one of us: 28 For in him we live, and move, and have our being; as certain also of your own poets have said, For we are also his offspring."
Acts 17:26-28

"But why dost thou judge thy brother? or why dost thou set at nought thy brother? for we shall all stand before the judgment seat of Christ."
Romans 14:10

"And there were dwelling at Jerusalem Jews, devout men, out of every nation under heaven. 6 Now when this was noised abroad, the multitude came together, and were confounded, because that every man heard them speak in his own language. 7 And they were all amazed and marvelled, saying one to another, Behold, are not all these which speak Galilaeans? 8 And how hear we every man in our own tongue, wherein we were born?"
Acts 2:5-8

Notes:

34

Turn Your Radio On

One Christmas when I was a teenager my parents gave me a crystal diode radio kit. The radio had to be assembled and then attached to an antenna wire before it would work. It is actually quite fun to listen to a radio that you build yourself.

Crystal diode radios are unique because they have no source of power in themselves...no electric cord and no battery. The secret to their operation is the crystal diode which is activated by the power of the radio waves from the station transmitter. Admittedly, the sound over the headphones is weak, but if one listens carefully the radio station can be fully enjoyed.

I had built my first *man cave* by the age of 14. I had model airplanes hanging from the ceiling, rocket posters on the wall, and a desk by my bed where I built my latest creations. I sat the crystal diode radio on my desk and would listen through the headphones as I worked.

There was one problem though, the radio would only pick up one station! Just outside of Grapevine and before they built DFW Airport there was an AM radio station. Since it was a couple of miles away it was the strongest signal and that is the only station I could hear. I think I heard Ray Charles sing, "Hit the Road Jack," several dozen times!

Inside the heart of man is a *radio* that can communicate with God. For most folks this radio is turned off. Actually, we can blame that on Adam.

When God made man he was created in perfection of body, soul, and spirit. It is the spirit of man that communicates with God. When man sinned against God that spirit within man died instantly. The radio was turned off. However, when a man or woman accepts Jesus Christ, the radio is again turned on.

We must be careful because even though we are receiving the signal from God, things in our human activities can drown out the signal. God gave us instruction as follows,

"Be still and know that I am God."
Psalm 46:10

It is up to us to take the time and listen carefully to what God is saying. How is that done? By simply taking the time to be still and read from the Bible, God's Holy Word.

Take time to read the Bible and learn the secrets of living an abundant life. Look at the examples of men and women recorded in Scripture that made mistakes so that we would not repeat them. There are examples of those who listened to God and wrought great success.

There was a time that the Prophet Elijah was discouraged and God told Elijah to stand on the mountain of God. Perhaps Elijah was looking for a sign from God, probably by some grandiose demonstration.

"And he said, Go forth, and stand upon the mount before the LORD. And, behold, the LORD passed by, and a great and strong wind rent the mountains, and brake in pieces the rocks before the LORD; but the LORD was not in the wind: and after the wind an earthquake; but the LORD was not in the earthquake: 12 And after the earthquake a fire; but the LORD was not in the fire: and after the fire a still small voice."
I Kings 19:11-12

The Bible says that God sent a mighty wind that was so strong that it broke stones, but God was not in the wind. God also sent an earthquake, and again God was not in the earthquake. Next God sent a fire, but God was not in the fire. Finally, there was a still small voice, and when Elijah heard it, he knew it was God speaking to him. His *radio* picked up the *signal* even though it was a still small voice.

"The Spirit itself beareth witness with our spirit, that we are the children of God."
Romans 8:16

It is imperative that we tune our spiritual radio to the Living Spirit of God for sweet communion with the Heavenly Father. Now that's what I call Divine programing!

Additional Scriptures

"Wherefore, my beloved brethren, let every man be swift to hear, slow to speak, slow to wrath:"
James 1:19

"Call unto me, and I will answer thee, and show thee great and mighty things, which thou knowest not."
Jeremiah 33:3

"But he said, Yea rather, blessed are they that hear the word of God, and keep it."
Luke 11:28

"Therefore whosoever heareth these sayings of mine, and doeth them, I will liken him unto a wise man, which built his house upon a rock: 25 And the rain descended, and the floods came, and the winds blew, and beat upon that house; and it fell not: for it was founded upon a rock."
Matthew 7:24-25

"But be ye doers of the word, and not hearers only,"
James 1:22

"And if we know that he hear us, whatsoever we ask, we know that we have the petitions that we desired of him."
I John 5:15

Notes:

35

Tried and Proven

Recently I heard the story of a missionary that worked with the American Indians, telling them about Jesus and how He died on the cross for their sins. One of the men in the tribe prayed the sinner's prayer and asked Jesus to come into his heart and forgive him of all his sins. The missionary then gave him a Bible and afterwards left to work in another area.

Some months passed by when the missionary went to check on the new convert. The Indian man enthusiastically showed the missionary his Bible. As the missionary scanned the pages he found that many scripture verses were underlined and had a "TP" written by the verse. A little confused by the "TP" marking the missionary asked the man what it meant. With a big smile the American Indian man said, "That means Tried and Proven."

We actually apply the principle of tried and proven to many areas of our lives. For example, if you have purchased a car recently what is the first thing you do before agreeing to buy the car? You take it for a test drive! That is the process of tried and proven. Another example is if you buy or rent a house. You will visit the property, going room by room to determine if the house will be suitable for your needs. Again, tried and proven!

God tells us in His Word that we should prove Him! That means to put God to the test and try Him.

"But my God shall supply all your need according to his riches in glory by Christ Jesus."
Philippians 4:19

There are two key phrases in this verse. First, *"your need"* is those things truly needed. God never intended to supply all your wants. Secondly, *"by Christ Jesus"* is the avenue by which God supplies needs. Jesus is the visible representation of the invisible God. The only way to God is thru Jesus.

"I can do all things through Christ which strengtheneth me."
Philippians 4:13

Paul could make this claim because he truly had tried and proven the goodness of God.
God also tries us and proves us.

"For thou, O God, hast proved us: thou hast tried us, as silver is tried."
Psalm 66:10

An interesting verse, but we are tried and proven the same as silver in the refiner's fire. The silver is purified and made fit for use by the fire. We too are tried and proven by God in fires of trial and affliction. God does not allow these things in our lives as punishment, but He allows trial and affliction to make us stronger. The fire removes the dross or impurities thus allowing us to be pure and fit for use.

Christian people who have been tried and proven in the refining fires of God are now fit to help others who are enduring similar trials. A person that has survived cancer can be of great comfort to someone else who has just discovered they too have cancer. The tried and proven have a purpose for the glory of God.

Finally, God told Israel in the book of Malachi to prove him by trusting Him and He would open the windows of heaven for a blessing so great it would be impossible to receive it all.

The LORD God is truly great. I recommend that you try and prove Him yourself. Trust in Him. You will be glad you did.

Additional Scriptures

"Bring ye all the tithes into the storehouse, that there may be meat in mine house, and prove me now herewith, saith the LORD of hosts, if I will not open you the windows of heaven, and pour you out a blessing, that there shall not be room enough to receive it."
Malachi 3:10

"Therefore say thou unto them, Thus saith the LORD of hosts; Turn ye unto me, saith the LORD of hosts, and I will turn unto you, saith the LORD of hosts."

Zechariah 1:3

"Return, ye backsliding children, and I will heal your backslidings. Behold, we come unto thee; for thou art the LORD our God."
Jeremiah 3:22

"But the word of the Lord endureth for ever. And this is the word which by the gospel is preached unto you."
I Peter 1:25

"Honour the LORD with thy substance, and with the firstfruits of all thine increase: 10 So shall thy barns be filled with plenty, and thy presses shall burst out with new wine."
Proverbs 3:9-10

"Upon the first day of the week let every one of you lay by him in store, as God hath prospered him, that there be no gatherings when I come."
I Corinthians 16:2

Notes:

36

The Life of a Dinosaur

If you ask the average person when dinosaurs lived on the earth the answer will probably be, *"Millions of years ago."* This answer has been taught in our schools and universities for a long time, so it is natural that's the answer you'll get.

Some of the first fossils of these great creatures were discovered in the early 1800's. Scientists didn't have much to go on in those days but they were very excited about these enormous animals.

The word *"dinosaur"* was coined by biologist and paleontologist Sir Richard Owen of England around 1841. The name stuck. You will not see the word *"dinosaur"* in the 1611 King James Version of the bible because the word was not invented until 230 years later!

If you were to ask me when dinosaurs lived on the earth I would tell you something completely contrary to what is accepted today. Just to mention the word *"dinosaur"* ignites a controversy between science and religion. Christian people will usually accept the explanation given by science or will avoid the subject all together. It's a shame that the church has not instilled a confidence within its parishioners regarding the subject. The narrative in the Bible is quite different from what the scientific community would say.

For me, it is not a matter of religion verses science, but rather my relationship with God and accepting by faith the narrative given to us in the Bible by the LORD God himself.

In the book of Hebrews chapter 11 and verse 3,

"Through faith we understand that the worlds were framed by the word of God, so that things which are seen were not made of things which do appear."

To begin with, we see here where God created all things by His command. It is by faith I believe that God created the dinosaurs on the sixth day of creation. One cannot deny that these creatures roamed the earth, but they did not roam alone.

"And God said, Let the earth bring forth the living creature after his kind, cattle, and creeping thing, and beast of the earth after his kind: and it was so."
Genesis 1:24

In this narrative God has, by simply speaking the command, created all land roaming creatures.

Now, the scientific community and the Hollywood animators always portray dinosaurs as savage beasts roaming the earth looking for their next meal. From an early age we are taught of the fierceness of the Tyrannosaurus Rex with the large gaping mouth filled with shark-like teeth being on the prowl, killing and eating everything in its path. These images capture the imagination and make good horror movies, but let's look at the Bible once again.

"And to every beast of the earth, and to every fowl of the air, and to every thing that creepeth upon the earth, wherein there is life, I have given every green herb for meat: and it was so."
Genesis 1:30

Did you see that? According to the Bible, God said that all life on the earth was to eat plants! Wow...the T-Rex was a vegetarian!

The word *"dinosaur"* is not in the Bible. But remember that from Hebrews chapter 11 and verse 3 and we believe by faith. Therefore in the book of Job and chapter 40 and verse 15-24 is a description of a huge land animal that I personally believe is the Brachiosaurus. It was God speaking to Job when he said,

"Behold now behemoth, which I made with you."

Since God pointed out the behemoth to Job we see where man and dinosaur are on the earth at the same time.

It is from passages like this in the Bible that I learn the greatness of God. He truly is all powerful and wise, all knowing of all things. So with great joy

I place my confidence in the LORD God, the Great and Strong Creator of all things.

Additional Scriptures

"And out of the ground the LORD God formed every beast of the field, and every fowl of the air; and brought them unto Adam to see what he would call them: and whatsoever Adam called every living creature, that was the name thereof. 20 And Adam gave names to all cattle, and to the fowl of the air, and to every beast of the field; but for Adam there was not found an help meet for him."
Genesis 2:19-20

"Or speak to the earth, and it shall teach thee: and the fishes of the sea shall declare unto thee. 9 Who knoweth not in all these that the hand of the LORD hath wrought this? 10 In whose hand is the soul of every living thing, and the breath of all mankind."
Job 12:8-10

"By his spirit he hath garnished the heavens; his hand hath formed the crooked serpent."
Job 26:13

"For by him were all things created, that are in heaven, and that are in earth, visible and invisible, whether they be thrones, or dominions, or principalities, or powers: all things were created by him, and for him:"
Colossians 1:16

"All things were made by him; and without him was not any thing made that was made."
John 1:3

"For thus saith the LORD that created the heavens; God himself that formed the earth and made it; he hath established it, he created it not in vain, he formed it to be inhabited: I am the LORD; and there is none else."
Isaiah 45:18

Notes:

37

The Day the Church Fell In

Bethel Baptist Church in Grapevine, Texas, where I grew up, is still an ongoing work for Christ. My dad retired from the pastorate in Grapevine about 12 years ago. While Dad was there the LORD blessed the work and it grew. During the 1960's the church entered into four building programs to enlarge the church campus.

The last project was the construction of an auditorium to hold all the people that came for services. The building had been framed and they thought they were ready for the roof trusses to span side wall to side wall. Long story short, the workmen had not used enough bracing on the side walls and while the trusses were hoisted into position the strain on the structure became enormous. All of a sudden, the trusses shifted and began to fall and domino to the ground. One man on top rode the trusses down. No one was seriously hurt, but one man got a broken finger in the event.

They say where there is smoke there is fire. The news of the event traveled fast in town and a constant stream of cars made the journey to our neighborhood to see the church that fell in. Then the news of the event became exaggerated...now the story was that three men were seriously hurt, one dead, and the preacher is missing. Dad was making a hospital call at the time. They say that a lie can travel around the world while the truth is lacing its shoes.

The truth of the Gospel of Jesus Christ is God's love towards man. It is interesting to me that people are more interested in a disaster at the church rather than going to hear the truth. I have heard about every excuse there is for not coming to church.

The church is the people, and people, while Christian, are still in the flesh and not perfect. Their spirit is holy through the blood of Jesus Christ. Perhaps someone unknowingly offended you. Perhaps someone has disappointed you. Perhaps the people became emotional for some reason. In either case, perhaps your church fell in. Discouraged, you are not willing to endure the agony of another service. Well, I know exactly what you are talking about. I am a preacher's kid and have endured about every scenario possible. Seems that preacher's kids endure the worst. Even when we are hurt, we have to go back!

The church is many things to many different people. For one thing, I believe the church is a place of worship and praise, and a place of healing and restoration. That's why I go. That's why I'm in the pastorate.

I don't advocate caving in the church building, but at the same time I would love for people to come just to hear encouraging words from Scripture and how great God really is. A. W. Tozer said that no religion will rise higher that the peoples' concept of God. My years as a preacher's kid and being a pastor myself, I think Tozer hit the nail on the head.

The Bible says in John chapter 4 and verse 24,

"They that worship God must
worship him in spirit and in truth."

The worship experience at church is not about you, it is about God. We come to approach His throne of grace and to learn about Him. It is not about me, it is not about you, it is about Him.

The event at Bethel Baptist Church passed on in time. The building was properly braced and the trusses were repaired and installed. The building was finished and Bethel Baptist has been worshiping in that place for over 45 years. It is still standing.

I hope you don't have a church building fall in order to pay us a visit. First Baptist Church in Roxton has been around for nearly 125 years. A Church is just people, and people make mistakes. I don't think the building ever fell in, and God is still on his throne.

Additional Scriptures

"How is it then, brethren? when ye come together,
every one of you hath a psalm, hath a doctrine,
hath a tongue, hath a revelation, hath an
interpretation. Let all things be done unto edifying."
I Corinthians 14:26

"Let all things be done decently and in order."
I Corinthians 14:40

"Let us walk honestly, as in the day; not in rioting and drunkenness, not in chambering and wantonness, not in strife and envying."
Romans 13:13

"This I say then, Walk in the Spirit, and ye shall not fulfil the lust of the flesh."
Galatians 5:16

"For they that are after the flesh do mind the things of the flesh; but they that are after the Spirit the things of the Spirit."
Romans 8:5

"There is therefore now no condemnation to them which are in Christ Jesus, who walk not after the flesh, but after the Spirit."
Romans 8:1

Notes:

38

Generations of Genealogies

One of the most challenging aspects of reading the Bible is working through all the genealogies. Seems like they go on and on, with names that are impossible to pronounce. The genealogies are particular in the Old Testament. It reads like this, "This guy begat that guy, and that guy begat another guy," and it makes you wonder what God was thinking when He inspired the scriptures to be written. Don't worry, God knew exactly what He was doing.

A popular pastime these days is digging around in your ancestry. I know who my grandparents were on my mother's side and my father's side, and that is about it. I recall meeting my great-grandmother once on my Dad's side of the family, but that was a very long time ago. She was a shriveled up old lady that wore a dark bonnet, and everyone called her, "Maw."

The genealogies in the Bible are there for a purpose. They are a gift so we would know the lineage of Jesus Christ. After the genealogies are listed in Matthew and Luke when Jesus was born they are never repeated in the Bible.

One of my favorite genealogies listed in the Bible is found in the book of Ruth. Ruth chapter 4 and verses 18-22,

"Now these are the generations of Pharez: Pharez begat Hezron, And Hezron begat Ram, and Ram begat Amminadab, And Amminadab begat Nahshon, and Nahshon begat Salmon, And Salmon begat Boaz, and Boaz begat Obed, And Obed begat Jesse, and Jesse begat David."

David became the King of Israel. Jesus Christ was born of the house and lineage of King David. Jesus was not born of royalty in a palace, but born a servant, laid in a manger of hay.

King David's great grandfather was Boaz which means his great grandmother was Ruth. I wonder if Ruth was still alive when David was on the throne. I guess we will find out in heaven.

Admittedly, the genealogies can be a tough read, but I think the key is to look for those tidbits of familiar names. The genealogies in Matthew Chapter one begins with Abraham. Abraham's son Isaac is familiar, as is Jacob and his son Judah. After Judah the names get vague until you get to David and Solomon. Yes, that is King Solomon. King of all Israel after his father David. Solomon built the Temple and passed the Kingdom on to his son Rehoboam. Under Rehoboam's rule Israel was divided in two parts...Rehoboam ruled over Judah and Benjamin, and Jeroboam ruled over the northern ten tribes of Israel, known as Israel. The line of Christ went through David the King, so His lineage went through the kings of Judah.

If one cares to read further, the book of First and Second Kings is the story of the Kings of Judah and Israel. Interestingly, all the Kings of Israel were considered bad kings because they encouraged idolatry for the people of Israel, which is against God's law. The Kings of Judah were better, for when they sought after God the Kingdom of Judah prospered, and when they sometime pursued idolatry, the kingdom was harassed by its enemies. The Kingdom of Judah would eventually fall under King Zedekiah. I think there is a lesson for us in that.

So the next time you read your Bible and come to the genealogies, don't give up and skip over them. God put them in His Word for our benefit. Look for the familiar names and follow the trail to the birth of Jesus Christ.

And remember that it is Jesus' blood that makes us part of the great heritage in the family of God. Remember that we are adopted into the family of God through Jesus Christ. Remember where Paul wrote in Romans chapter 8 and verse 15,

"For ye have not received the spirit of bondage again to fear; but ye have received the Spirit of adoption, whereby we cry, Abba, Father."

It is because of Jesus Christ that our names are written in the Book of Life (Revelation 20:15). We are now in covenant with God. We are now family. Generations.

Additional Scriptures

"But when the fulness of the time was come, God sent forth his Son, made of a woman, made under the law, 5 To redeem them that were under the law, that we might receive the adoption of sons."
Galatians 4:4-5

"And saying, The time is fulfilled, and the kingdom of God is at hand: repent ye, and believe the gospel."
Mark 1:15

"That in the dispensation of the fulness of times he might gather together in one all things in Christ, both which are in heaven, and which are on earth; even in him:"
Ephesians 1:10

"And the angel answered and said unto her, The Holy Ghost shall come upon thee, and the power of the Highest shall overshadow thee: therefore also that holy thing which shall be born of thee shall be called the Son of God."
Luke 1:35

"And the Word was made flesh, and dwelt among us, (and we beheld his glory, the glory as of the only begotten of the Father,) full of grace and truth."
John 1:14

"In the beginning was the Word, and the Word was with God, and the Word was God."
John 1:1

Notes:

39

Faster Than the Speed of Light

Light is fast. I mean really fast. However, when one considers the vastness of the universe, light is really slow.

For the record, light travels at 186,282 miles per second. That means that if you could travel around the earth at the speed of light, you would circle the earth about 7.5 times in one second. That would be a quick trip without much time for sight-seeing. However, if you wanted to travel to the sun at the speed of light for a balmy vacation, the trip would take about 8 minutes. The sun is that far away.

In the early days of science, it was thought that light was instantaneous. As scientific measurements became possible, it was determined that light traveled at 186 thousand miles per second. For comparison, the moon is about 250 thousand miles from the earth so light takes about 1.3 seconds to make the trip.

The stars of light are so far away from the earth that we measure the distance from the earth to the stars in light-years. That means we multiply the speed of light by 60 seconds, and by 60 minutes, then 24 hours, then 365 days, and then years. If you are interested in a large number, light travels 5,878,499,810,000 miles in one year. Written out, that is 5 trillion, eight hundred and seventy eight billion, four hundred and ninety-nine million, and eight hundred and ten thousand miles. Whew!

When God created the sun, moon, and stars on the fourth day of creation He commanded that their light would shine upon the earth. Notice how He commanded in Genesis:

"And let them be for lights in the firmament of the heaven to give light upon the earth: and it was so. 16 And God made two great lights; the greater light to rule the day, and the lesser light to rule the night: he made the stars also."
Genesis 1:15-16

"By the word of the LORD were the heavens made; and all the host of them by the breath of his mouth. 9 For he spake, and it was done; he commanded, and it stood fast."
Psalm 33:6 and 9

So there it is. God commanded the stars to be in their position in space and then commanded their light to shine on the earth. In short, God broke the speed of light.

So for that reason, we can see stars that are millions of light years away from the earth. This might seem impossible, but remember that God is all powerful. In the study of Theology we call that "omnipotent."

Scientist have a hard time with the notion that God created all things from nothing, but He did. How do I know? The Bible tells me so.

"Through faith we understand that the worlds were framed (or made) by the word of God, so that things which are seen were not made of things which do appear."
Hebrews 11:3

In other words, God made everything from nothing.

"The LORD by wisdom hath founded the earth; by understanding hath he established the heavens."
Proverbs 3:19

This tells me that there is order to the universe because the LORD made it that way. Did you know that Abraham could see the same stars that we do today? So did Jesus, Paul, and Peter.

And God knew, in His infinite wisdom, that it would be necessary to break the speed of light for the light of the stars to be seen from earth.

God Himself is eternal, meaning that He had no beginning and will have no ending.

"Before the mountains were brought forth, or ever thou hadst formed the earth and the world, even from everlasting to everlasting, thou art God."
Psalm 90:2

Finally, the matter of breaking the light barrier, I want you to think on this. God broke the light barrier easier than you could open your own window shades at home.

"It is he that sitteth upon the circle of the earth, and the inhabitants thereof are as grasshoppers; that stretcheth out the heavens as a curtain, and spreadeth them out as a tent to dwell in:"
Isaiah 40:22

Not a problem for the Omnipotent God.

Additional Scriptures

"And God said, Let there be light: and there was light. 4 And God saw the light, that it was good: and God divided the light from the darkness. 5 And God called the light Day, and the darkness he called Night. And the evening and the morning were the first day."
Genesis 1:3-5

"And God said, Let there be lights in the firmament of the heaven to divide the day from the night; and let them be for signs, and for seasons, and for days, and years: 15 And let them be for lights in the firmament of the heaven to give light upon the earth: and it was so. 16 And God made two great lights; the greater light to rule the day, and the lesser light to rule the night: he made the stars also.

17 And God set them in the firmament of the heaven to give light upon the earth, 18 And to rule over the day and over the night, and to divide the light from the darkness: and God saw that it was good. 19 And the evening and the morning were the fourth day."
Genesis 1:14-19

"Thus saith God the LORD, he that created the heavens, and stretched them out; he that spread forth the earth, and that which cometh out of it; he that giveth breath unto the people upon it, and spirit to them that walk therein:"
Isaiah 42:5

"I have made the earth, and created man upon it: I, even my hands, have stretched out the heavens, and all their host have I commanded."
Isaiah 45:12

"Thus saith the LORD, which giveth the sun for a light by day, and the ordinances of the moon and of the stars for a light by night, which divideth the sea when the waves thereof roar; The LORD of hosts is his name:"
Jeremiah 31:35

"He telleth the number of the stars; he calleth them all by their names."
Psalm 147:4

Notes:

40

A Fearful Waste of Time

I like to watch the old western shows when possible. *Gunsmoke* was a cultural favorite. I remember watching shows after school like *The Rifleman, The Lone Ranger*, and *The Cisco Kid*. These shows and others were a real treasure in those days. And yes, the good guys always wore white hats.

On one western show there was a young boy that did not want to go to school. His Pa was encouraging him to go. The boy looked up at this Pa and said, "But Pa, it's a fearful waste of time." He probably figured that he did not need an education to punch cows and fight Indians.

We humans waste a fearful amount of time. God placed us on this earth for His glory. Our every effort should be directed at praising God in worship. The Psalmist David wrote in Psalm 34 and verse 1,

"I will bless the LORD at all times: his praise shall continually be in my mouth."

Solomon wrote in Ecclesiastes 3 that there is a time for everything. Paraphrased it says;

"There is a time to be born, a time to die, plant, harvest, kill, heal, break down, build up, to weep, laugh, mourn, and dance, a time to keep, a time to lose, to cast away, a time to rend, and sew,

a time to keep silence, and a time to speak. We also have time to love and hate, a time for war and a time for peace."

In all of these things we can keep the LORD God at the front of our mind and praise Him.

However we are a self-absorbed people that do many things without consulting the LORD God first. We take far too little time to read the Bible, far too little time in prayer. We make major life decisions without consulting the LORD God. As we face life we do so without the benefit of the wisdom of the LORD, and therefore we are on our own. The Apostle Paul encouraged us to use time wisely in Ephesians chapter 5 and verse 16,

"Redeeming the time, because the days are evil."

I believe the Apostle Paul meant that we should make the best use of our time, because a minute that is past is a minute gone forever. And because we are human there are moments of time that will slip away wasted, and not used efficiently. A fearful waste of time.

There is much encouragement in the Word of God about how we utilize time. David's prayer in Psalm 90 and verse 12:

"So teach us to number our days,
that we may apply our hearts unto wisdom."

Truth is, our lives are very short. It has been compared to a vapor that you can only see for a moment. The Apostle James wrote in chapter 4 and verse 14,

"Whereas ye know not what shall be on the morrow. For what is your life? It is even a vapour, that appeareth for a little time, and then vanisheth away."

When you have a chance, put some water on to boil. You will notice that the vapor of steam rises and is quickly absorbed into the air. You will also notice that the steam is stronger closer to the surface of the boiling water, and gets weaker as it moves upward. So is your life. You are the strongest when you are young.

I close with a verse that the Apostle Paul wrote in his letter to the church as Colossae. In Colossians 4 and verse 5,

"Walk in wisdom toward them that are without, redeeming the time."

We are to walk in wisdom as a demonstration of God's love to those that might not believe, or to those who might be considering joining with us for Worship.

The time is short. Don't waste it. You only have one chance to make a first impression.

Additional Scriptures

"LORD, make me to know mine end, and the measure of my days, what it is; that I may know how frail I am.5 Behold, thou hast made my days as an handbreadth; and mine age is as nothing before thee: verily every man at his best state is altogether vanity. Selah."
Psalm 39:4-5

"See then that ye walk circumspectly, not as fools, but as wise, 16 Redeeming the time, because the days are evil. 17 Wherefore be ye not unwise, but understanding what the will of the Lord is."
Ephesians 5:15-17

"Walk in wisdom toward them that are without, redeeming the time. 6 Let your speech be alway with grace, seasoned with salt, that ye may know how ye ought to answer every man."
Colossians 4:5-6

"And have no fellowship with the unfruitful works of darkness, but rather reprove them."
Ephesians 5:11

"Wherefore seeing we also are compassed about with so great a cloud of witnesses, let us lay aside every weight, and the sin which doth so easily beset us, and let us run with patience the race that is set before us, 2 Looking unto Jesus the author and

*finisher of our faith; who for the joy that was set
before him endured the cross, despising the shame,
and is set down at the right hand of the throne of
God."*
Hebrew 12:1-2

*"He is in the way of life that keepeth instruction:
but he that refuseth reproof erreth."*
Proverbs 10:17

Notes:

41

A Voice of Experience

When my son, Eric, was in the Navy we made a road trip from Fort Worth to San Diego to see him for Christmas in 2005. It was our first time to be that far west and to see the Pacific Ocean.

At the time I owned a 1986 Cadillac which I had purchased from a friend some years earlier. Even though it was high mileage, it was a good car with a nice ride and acceptable mileage on the road.

On our return trip back to Texas we decided to take some pictures of the sequoia cactuses in southern Arizona. Those cactuses are huge! I remember watching episodes of The Lone Ranger and The Cisco Kid with those cactuses in the scenery.

We stopped a couple of times to take pictures and never had any problems. Then we stopped a third time, took some pictures, and when we were ready to resume our trip the car would not start. Being the independent and resourceful guy that I am I tried everything I knew to get that car to start. It was not my day.

So here we are in southern Arizona on an interstate highway, the car won't start, and the sun is going down. My wife Jan suggested that we call the help line in the owner's manual of the car. I relented and we called the number. We were fortunate to have a cell phone signal in such a desolate place. The representative with Cadillac sent a wrecker to rescue us.

The next day, the repair shop determined the fuel pump needed to be replaced. As with most cars these days, the fuel pump is in the gas tank, so it not an easy job. You have to empty the gas out of the tank, then remove the gas tank from the car, then replace the pump in the tank. The young mechanic and his father were working feverishly knowing we were anxious to get back to Texas. When the young mechanic installed the new fuel pump his father told him to use the old rubber seal from the old fuel pump. "If you don't, it will leak," the old mechanic said. The young mechanic either did not listen or did not believe him and he installed the new pump with the new rubber seal.

They re-installed the gas tank and refilled the tank with gas. When it was full, gasoline poured out of the top of the tank and on to the ground. My heart sank. That meant the gas had to be drained again, the gas tank removed, and the leak resolved. Sure enough, it was the new rubber seal that leaked. Once the old seal was installed everything was fine. It pays to listen to the voice of experience!

I find that the voice of experience from the Bible gives us many examples on how to live an abundant life. From Noah, to Moses, to David, to Daniel, all these men found favor with God and their lives prospered as they obeyed the voice of the LORD God. The Bible says in I Corinthians chapter 10 and verse 6 that,

"these are given as examples."

And sure enough, they are there...good and bad. Jonah did not obey God and he ended up in the belly of a whale. King Zedekiah did not listen to the prophet Jeremiah and he lost his kingdom, his sons, and his eyesight.

Sometimes I think there is a hormone released in humans that prevents us from listening to the voice of experience. And the devil likes that, for he knows that as long as we do not listen to God, that he has the upper hand.

It's not likely for most of you, but if you ever find yourself in Roxton, Texas on a Sunday I hope you will visit with us at First Baptist Church. It would be a pleasure to have you there.

Additional Scriptures

"With the ancient is wisdom; and in length of days understanding."
Job 12:12

"And Elihu the son of Barachel the Buzite answered and said, I am young, and ye are very old; wherefore I was afraid, and durst not shew you mine opinion.
I said, Days should speak, and multitude of years should teach wisdom."
Job 32:6-7

"I have been young, and now am old; yet have I not

seen the righteous forsaken, nor his seed begging
bread."
Psalm 37:25

"Thou wilt shew me the path of life: in thy presence
is fulness of joy; at thy right hand there are
pleasures for evermore."
Psalm 16:11

"And not only so, but we glory in tribulations also:
knowing that tribulation worketh patience; 4 And
patience, experience; and experience, hope:
5 And hope maketh not ashamed; because the love
of God is shed abroad in our hearts by the Holy
Ghost which is given unto us."
Romans 5:3-5

"Whoso is wise, and will observe these things, even
they shall understand the lovingkindness of the
LORD."
Psalm 107:43

Notes:

42

Business at an Old-Fashioned Altar

Many moons ago I heard a joke about a church that had a revival meeting. The pastor of the church noticed that the town gossip came to the meeting, so he advised the evangelist that she was there. Since this was a rare opportunity the evangelist preached hard and thorough on the sin of gossiping.

An altar call was given and to the delight of the pastor and the evangelist the town gossip, obviously moved by the sermon, came forward. She went directly to the pastor and said, "Pastor, do you know I am the town gossip?"

"Yes Ma'am," he said.

Then with tears in her eyes she said "I am so convicted of the sin of gossiping that I would just like to lay my tongue on the altar."

The pastor replied, "Well Ma'am, the altar is over 14 feet long...just do the best you can!"

I remember as a child attending services in the old church building in Grapevine. The building was not air-conditioned, we had pine wood floors, the pews were made from regular dimensional lumber, and the people would respond to the preaching of the Gospel. It was not uncommon for several people to be moved by the preaching and walk the aisles to do business with God at the altar. Sinners would be converted to the Gospel, sins would be confessed, prayers offered for others, and people would make a fresh and new dedication of their lives to live for God.

It's not that way anymore. It is quite rare to see people humble themselves before God and pray at the church altar. Perhaps it is a matter of pride, but I do know that today we are not as committed to our God and His church.

For every believer in Christ, doing business with God at an altar is a life-long business. Jesus commanded men to always pray and not to faint. In the book of Luke chapter 18 and verse 1 Jesus said,

"that men ought always to pray, and not to faint".

Paul also admonished all believers to pray in the book of First Thessalonians chapter 5 and verse 17,

"Pray without ceasing."

Just as you would not take your car on a long journey without first filling it with gasoline, Christians too need the filling from God through prayer for life's journey.

The Bible says in Hebrews that Jesus Christ is the same; yesterday, today, and forever. Since God and His Christ do not change, the problem must lay with us. It is us that have made our hearts hardened to the Gospel making us unyielding and unresponsive to the wooing of the Holy Spirit. It is us that allows the sin of pride to keep us from humbling ourselves at an old fashioned altar to do serious business with God.

I would like to encourage you with words from the Apostle Paul which he said in Hebrews chapter 12 and verses 1 and 2,

"Wherefore seeing we also are compassed about with so great a cloud of witnesses, let us lay aside every weight, and the sin which doth so easily beset us, and let us run with patience the race that is set before us, 2 Looking unto Jesus the author and finisher of our faith; who for the joy that was set before him endured the cross, despising the shame, and is set down at the right hand of the throne of God."

Jesus humbled himself on the cross, endured horrific pain, endured unbelievable shame, and then died on the cross for our sins. For me it is unimaginable. Seeing what Jesus did for us should spur us on to do business with God at the church altar.

The next time you are in church and your heart is moved by the preaching of the Word, make a move at the invitation. Go the altar and do business with God.

Additional Scriptures

"And Moses built an altar, and called the name of it Jehovah-nissi: (The LORD is my Banner).

Exodus 17:15

"And it came to pass on the morrow, that the people rose early, and built there an altar, and offered burnt offerings and peace offerings."
Judges 21:4

"Wherefore lay apart all filthiness and superfluity of naughtiness, and receive with meekness the engrafted word, which is able to save your souls."
James 1:21

"Circumcise yourselves to the LORD, and take away the foreskins of your heart, ye men of Judah and inhabitants of Jerusalem: lest my fury come forth like fire, and burn that none can quench it, because of the evil of your doings."
Jeremiah 4:4

"For I am not ashamed of the gospel of Christ: for it is the power of God unto salvation to every one that believeth; to the Jew first, and also to the Greek."
Romans 1:16

"For the scripture saith, Whosoever believeth on him shall not be ashamed."
Romans 10:11

Notes:

43

Curley's Dirty Words

There's a stigma, a passage of right, when young people finally start to use *dirty* words. Personally, I hear a lot of it since I work with grown men in the electric industry. Many of the jobs they do are hard with adverse weather, muddy ground, and trees tangled in our electric wires. Sometimes it can be a real mess. I usually hear the expletives cascade down the hall to my office. I then know they will have to deal with a very messy situation in the field that day.

I always admired an episode of The Three Stooges where the Stooges were witnesses in court. The Bailiff tried to swear in Curley to the witness stand. Curley is probably the best loved stooge as he would do his funny antics, sometimes falling to the floor and doing a spin. The reasons he would drop to the floor is that he forgot his lines. The spins would make people laugh so the director would leave them in the movie.

Anyway, the Bailiff is giving Curley the oath, but the bailiff is speaking so fast that Curley can't understand him. Frustrated, the bailiff repeats the oath, and Curley still does not understand. So the judge interrupts the bailiff and asked Curley, "Do you swear to…" Curley quickly responds with his childish manner… "No, but I know all the words!"

Man has twisted some words and made up others to have a verbiage used to insult others and vent their frustrations. Language is a precious gift from God. Cursing, on the other hand, is language that is offensive. It is no different than passing gas in a public place or peeing in a swimming pool. All these things are offensive and you should not do them.

Profanity itself is selfish and self-centered. Not caring about the feelings of other people or what they think is the most selfish of all. Swearing is the act of a lazy mind, not thinking as poor words of expression are chosen. As a pastor I know the importance of choosing my words wisely for each sermon. That is why I study and make guide notes…it is preparation to explain the truth of the Bible as precisely as possible.

I have an Amazon Parrot hen named Kash. Jan and I adopted her about 10 years ago. Kash and I have grown close. She likes to be with me when I am around the house, and she has just about lost her bad habit of cursing. When we adopted her, she could really use some choice words. Kash still talks, but when we first got her she could really make a sailor blush with some of her words. Her previous owners thought it was funny for a bird to cuss. Jan and I do not speak that way, and over the years Kash has pretty much forgotten her torrid past.

The truth is, Kash does not know the meaning of the words, and she just repeats what she has heard. Her favorite words are, *"Hungry, Hello, and*

What." Every once in a while she will slip and we hear $#@% and &%$%@. Oh well, we have tried.

So, what does God say in all this? He made this simple for you and me as Jesus Christ spoke in Matthew chapter 5 and verses 34-37,

"But I say unto you, Swear not at all; neither by heaven; for it is God's throne: Nor by the earth; for it is his footstool: neither by Jerusalem; for it is the city of the great King. Neither shalt thou swear by thy head, because thou canst not make one hair white or black. But let your communication be, Yea, yea; Nay, nay: for whatsoever is more than these cometh of evil."

So there it is. Jesus said we are not to swear at all. If you can't think of anything better to say, a simple Yes or No will do nicely. The risk of being offensive is much less and we will be the happier for it.

Additional Scriptures

"But now ye also put off all these; anger, wrath, malice, blasphemy, filthy communication out of your mouth."
Colossians 3:8

"Let no corrupt communication proceed out of your mouth, but that which is good to the use of edifying, that it may minister grace unto the hearers."

Ephesians 4:29

"And he called the multitude, and said unto them, Hear, and understand:
11 Not that which goeth into the mouth defileth a man; but that which cometh out of the mouth, this defileth a man."
Matthew 15:10-11

"Out of the same mouth proceedeth blessing and cursing. My brethren, these things ought not so to be. 11 Doth a fountain send forth at the same place sweet water and bitter? 12 Can the fig tree, my brethren, bear olive berries? either a vine, figs? so can no fountain both yield salt water and fresh.13 Who is a wise man and endued with knowledge among you? let him shew out of a good conversation his works with meekness of wisdom."
James 3:10-13

"Whoso keepeth his mouth and his tongue keepeth his soul from troubles."
Proverbs 21:23

"If any man among you seem to be religious, and bridleth not his tongue, but deceiveth his own heart, this man's religion is vain."
James 1:26

Notes:

44

To Give a Man a Fish

There's an old saying out there: "Give a man a fish, and he can eat for a day. Teach a man to fish and he can eat for a lifetime."

When our family moved in 1962 to the parsonage behind Bethel Baptist Church, We left behind a comfortable way of life. Dad had a good job in the aircraft industry as a chrome plater. We lived in a moderately priced house. I remember the beautiful St. Augustine lawn and shade trees. Life was good. We had a nice car, and there was always food on the table.

The parsonage at Bethel Baptist Church was quite small. It was uninsulated, unfinished, and the only source of heat was a Dearborn heater in the living room. The cabinets in the kitchen were wooden crates nailed to the wall. We would stay near the Dearborn heater to stay warm as Mom figured out a way to get meals on the table.

Dad's salary was meager so he supplemented his income by using his savings account for cash. There were also a few men in the church that would go fishing at the nearby lake and would give their catch to the preacher of the church. Dad would clean the fish, Mom would fry them, and we would have fresh fish for supper.

Dad decided to start fishing himself, and we would frequently go to the lake for a family picnic and some fishing. We fished with cane poles in still waters and we usually caught a few, usually enough for another fried fish supper.

If Dad had just waited for the men of the church to come by to give us their catch, there could have been days we went hungry. But because Dad started fishing himself with the men of the church giving advice on where the fish are biting and what bait to use, we could eat fish most any time we wanted.

A typical service at First Baptist Church will feature reading the Word of God. We will sing, we will pray and we will preach. Preaching is simply an explanation of the Bible.

If you are ever in Roxton, Texas I hope you will come and join with us, but if you are depending on the church service for all the *religion* you get in a week you will not get all you really need for the week. As a pastor I encourage you to spend time in the Word of God yourself all through the week.

For example, my mother will read a chapter from the book of Proverbs every day. Proverbs has 31 chapters, so it can be easily read in a month. The chapters are not that long, and can be read by the average reader in just a couple of minutes. Proverbs has much wisdom, it is not deep at all, and it will really enhance your life.

So between the reading and study at home and the services at your church, your spiritual *tank* will be fuller as you live day to day.

Finally, wisdom from The Apostle Paul...In

II Timothy chapter 2 and verse 15,

"Study to shew thyself approved unto God, a workman that needeth not to be ashamed, rightly dividing the word of truth."

The study that the preacher does in preparation for Sunday service and his preaching is only a part of your Christian life. You need to read and study for yourself. It's OK for it to take some time, study at your own pace. There could be a test later.

Additional Scriptures

"I will meditate in thy precepts, and have respect unto thy ways. 16 I will delight myself in thy statutes: I will not forget thy word."
Psalm 119:15-16

"For Ezra had prepared his heart to seek the law of the LORD, and to do it, and to teach in Israel statutes and judgments."
Ezra 7:10

"This book of the law shall not depart out of thy mouth; but thou shalt meditate therein day and night, that thou mayest observe to do according to all that is written therein: for then thou shalt make thy way prosperous, and then thou shalt have good success."

Joshua 1:8

"Hear, O my son, and receive my sayings; and the years of thy life shall be many. 11 I have taught thee in the way of wisdom; I have led thee in right paths. 12 When thou goest, thy steps shall not be straitened; and when thou runnest, thou shalt not stumble. 13 Take fast hold of instruction; let her not go: keep her; for she is thy life."
Proverbs 4:10-13

"These were more noble than those in Thessalonica, in that they received the word with all readiness of mind, and searched the scriptures daily, whether those things were so."
Acts 17:11

"All scripture is given by inspiration of God, and is profitable for doctrine, for reproof, for correction, for instruction in righteousness: 17 That the man of God may be perfect, thoroughly furnished unto all good works."
II Timothy 3:16-17

Notes:

45

How to Make a Big Boo-boo

When Bethel Baptist Church in Grapevine launched its fourth building program in the 1960's, it was a big deal for the church. It was also a big deal for the general contractor doing the work. A lot of money was at stake and there was a deadline to meet.

Shortly after the ground breaking ceremony, a group of trucks came to dig the piers for the foundation. It's interesting, that every pier sits on solid rock. That building has not moved. Then the workmen installed the forms for the foundation. I don't know why the contractor did so, but the decision was made to pour the foundation as a storm front moved in. It was a big boo-boo.

The concrete was poured and the workmen began smoothing the slab. Then, it began to rain. The falling rain ruined the finish on the concrete so the men had to keep working the concrete for it to be smooth. As soon as they smoothed the concrete, it would rain again.

The slab had a slope in it towards the front of the building and that low place filled with water from the rain. The contractor had no choice but to knock a hole in the forms to allow the water to drain out. The men would smooth the concrete once again, and then it would rain again.

The loss of the foundation slab would mean economic disaster for the contractor and a huge setback for the church, so the men were required to keep working, a break was not allowed. My Dad felt sorry for the men, knowing they were doing all they could to save the slab. They were tired, hungry, and wet. Dad decided to take action, so he went to Mom.

I can almost hear him now, "Honey, is there *anything* we can give those men to eat?" My mother is the master at finding a meal when it seems impossible. When she was a young girl on the farm she would make biscuits and gravy for the men at breakfast. In fact, the first breakfast she fixed my Dad you could have fed Cox's Army. I think she fixed Dad about three dozen biscuits and a gallon of gravy. Obviously, she would have to make some adjustments.

First, Mom put on a pot of coffee. Next, all she could find in the pantry was a can of Spam and a can of whole kernel corn. She mixed up a big batch of cornbread and diced that can of spam into small chunks and added the Spam and the drained can of corn to the mix. She then made "pancakes" in the skillet and took that food to those tired and wet men. When you are hungry anything will do and those men would hold those Spam corncakes in one hand and eat while operating the smoothing machines with the other hand. The men were fed, they worked the slab all night, and the slab was saved.

If the contractor had consulted the weatherman he could have prevented his mistake. Luke chapter 14 and verse 28,

"For which of you, intending to build a tower, sitteth not down first, and counteth the cost, whether he have sufficient to finish it?"

The consideration of the weather was a serious cost that the contractor did not think through.

In all aspects of our lives we need to consider the cost of what we plan to do. It doesn't matter if you plan to change jobs or build a room onto the house. What is the impact on your life? What is the impact on your wife and children? Will I have enough money to finish the project? Will I have enough time to finish the project? Will the work bring a satisfaction to my life? Will this project honor God?

I was just a young and hungry teenager at the time, I think I snatched one of those *Spam-corncakes* for myself. The best I can remember, it was pretty good.

Additional Scriptures

"Fear thou not; for I am with thee: be not dismayed; for I am thy God: I will strengthen thee; yea, I will help thee; yea, I will uphold thee with the right hand of my righteousness."
Isaiah 41:10

"Though he fall, he shall not be utterly cast down:
for the LORD upholdeth him with his hand."
Psalm 37:24

"Humble yourselves therefore under the mighty
hand of God, that he may exalt you in due time: 7
Casting all your care upon him; for he careth for
you."
I Peter 5:6-7

"Judge not, that ye be not judged."
Matthew 7:1

"And it shall come to pass, if thou shalt hearken
diligently unto the voice of the LORD thy God, to
observe and to do all his commandments which I
command thee this day, that the LORD thy God will
set thee on high above all nations of the earth: 2
And all these blessings shall come on thee, and
overtake thee, if thou shalt hearken unto the voice
of the LORD thy God."
Deuteronomy 28:1-2

"But they that wait upon the LORD shall renew their
strength; they shall mount up with wings as eagles;
they shall run, and not be weary; and they shall
walk, and not faint."
Isaiah 40:31

Notes:

46

The Doomsday Seed Vault

Deep in the snow covered mountains of a Norwegian island is a huge vault that houses seeds from virtually every country for many known plants. The technical name for the vault is The Svalbard Global Seed Vault. It is there in the event that seeds are needed for humans to replace their vegetation.

Seeds are stored in a safe deposit box of sorts for each country. The country that sent the seeds retains ownership. The seeds are stored in four ply plastic bags and the vault is kept at a negative 18 centigrade, or just about zero degrees Fahrenheit. The low temperatures extend the life of the seeds.

The country of Norway owns the facility, but the expense of operating the vault is shared by Norway and the Global Crop Diversity Trust. In the history of the vault, only one country has made a withdrawal. Due to the civil war, Syria has withdrawn seeds.

I can see a time that many countries will want to withdraw seeds to establish crops, and that will be during the time that God will judge this earth. In fact, because of God's judgement, most systems of transportation will not be usable, so man might not be able to redistribute the seeds to their owners.

The Bible says in Revelation chapter 8 and verse 7,

"The first angel sounded, and there followed hail and fire mingled with blood, and they were cast upon the earth: and the third part of trees was burnt up, and all green grass was burnt up."

This first event will be horrific. Imagine the entire planet is engulfed in flames from the hail and fire beating down plant life and fire burning a third of all trees in the forest and all grass. I would imagine that included any crops that are planted. Many houses will be lost to the fire. There will be nothing firefighters can do since the scope of the disaster will be so great. The smoke will cover the planet.

Next, the second angel sounds a judgment in Revelation 8:8-9,

"And the second angel sounded, and as it were a great mountain burning with fire was cast into the sea: and the third part of the sea became blood; 9 And the third part of the creatures which were in the sea, and had life, died; and the third part of the ships were destroyed."

It might be that a huge asteroid like object enters the atmosphere, is burning, and hits the oceans. The Creator God is judging this earth, and the Sovereign causes a third of the oceans to turn to blood, the Omnipotent God can make that happen. I know, it sounds gross. But as a result, one third of the aquatic life will die. The carcasses of millions of animals of all types will wash up on the beaches.

People will still be dealing with the impact of the loss of trees and grass, and now this ecological disaster is so great there is nothing they can do. The stench of dying flesh will fill the air with the smoke of the grass and trees. And the economic disaster from the loss of the ships will be incredible.

The third angel sounds judgment in Revelation chapter 8 and verses 10-11,

"10 And the third angel sounded, and there fell a great star from heaven, burning as it were a lamp, and it fell upon the third part of the rivers, and upon the fountains of waters; 11 And the name of the star is called Wormwood: and the third part of the waters became wormwood; and many men died of the waters, because they were made bitter."

The second judgment was directed at the salt waters of the earth. The third judgment is directed at a third of the fresh waters of the earth. Have you ever been thirsty? Imagine the difficulty of getting a glass of fresh, cool clean water. Your throat becomes powdery dry. Nothing else will refresh, and no fresh water is available. God is judging this earth.

Finally, the fourth angel sounds judgment in Revelation chapter 8 and verse 12,

"And the fourth angel sounded, and the third part of the sun was smitten, and the third part of the moon, and the third part of the stars; so as the third

part of them was darkened, and the day shone not for a third part of it, and the night likewise."

I am going to the edge here, but I believe that God will speed up the rotation of the earth where it only takes 16 hours for a day and a night. And not the usual 24 hours. And if that is true, it will be impossible for the seeds from the Doomsday vault to grow and mature because there is not enough daylight for the seeds to grow. The biological clock of the people of the world will go haywire too.

The Doomsday Vault is a good idea, but when God judges this earth on Doomsday, the Vault will become null and void.

Additional Scriptures

"For promotion cometh neither from the east, nor from the west, nor from the south. 7 But God is the judge: he putteth down one, and setteth up another."
Psalm 75:6-7

"And the heavens shall declare his righteousness: for God is judge himself. Selah."
Psalm 50:6

"For by fire and by his sword will the LORD plead with all flesh: and the slain of the LORD shall be many."
Isaiah 66:16

"And Abraham drew near, and said, Wilt thou also destroy the righteous with the wicked? 24 Peradventure there be fifty righteous within the city: wilt thou also destroy and not spare the place for the fifty righteous that are therein? 25 That be far from thee to do after this manner, to slay the righteous with the wicked: and that the righteous should be as the wicked, that be far from thee: Shall not the Judge of all the earth do right? 26 And the LORD said, If I find in Sodom fifty righteous within the city, then I will spare all the place for their sakes."
Genesis 18:23-26

"Therefore wait ye upon me, saith the LORD, until the day that I rise up to the prey: for my determination is to gather the nations, that I may assemble the kingdoms, to pour upon them mine indignation, even all my fierce anger: for all the earth shall be devoured with the fire of my jealousy."
Zephaniah 3:8

"For we know him that hath said, Vengeance belongeth unto me, I will recompense, saith the Lord. And again, The Lord shall judge his people. 31 It is a fearful thing to fall into the hands of the living God."
Hebrews 10:30-31

Notes:

47

The Gift of Gideon

The biblical narrative of Gideon is a fascinating study. Gideon lived during a time when Israel did not have a King. Israel would disobey God and God would allow an enemy to harass them in some way. God would raise up *judges* to provide deliverance.

In Gideon's day, Israel had disobeyed and God allowed the Midianites to invade the land. The book of Judges Chapter 6 verse 1,

"And the children of Israel did evil in the sight of the LORD: and the LORD delivered them into the hand of Midian seven years."

One thing the Midianites would do is to take the crops of food away from Israel. That's where we find Gideon. He is threshing grain in a hiding place so that the Midianites will not take his grain. Then the Angel of the LORD appears to Gideon and calls Gideon, *"A mighty man of valor."* Truth is, Gideon was a mighty man of valor, but Gideon didn't think so.

Gideon told the angel that he was from a poor family of the tribe of Manasseh, and that Gideon was the least of his father's house. Gideon did not think himself to be of any significance.

God specializes in using people of low estate to accomplish great works in His name. The Bible doesn't say that Noah was rich or had any position, but it does say that Noah had a relationship with God. It takes a lot of faith to build a giant barge on dry land when it has never rained. But Noah believed God and built the ark.

The prophet Elijah was a *nobody*, from nowhere. The Bible calls Elijah, "Elijah the Tishbite," but no one really knows where Tisbeh is on the map. The Bible gives us the picture of a man that is rough with a leather belt about his waist.

John the Baptist also was a rough character that ate locust and wild honey. Another nobody from nowhere.

The gift that Gideon had is that he knew where he came from, that he was small, he held no position, and that God would use him to accomplish a great purpose. Gideon used his nothingness for the glory of the great God. Gideon gathered thirty-two thousand men to fight with Midian, but God said that was too many. God did not allow Israel to think that theirs was the victory when God was fighting for them, so there was a simple test. God told Gideon to announce that if anyone was afraid or fearful that they could go home. Of the thirty-two thousand there, twenty two thousand went home. Now Gideon had ten thousand to fight the battle.

In all things we are to give God the honor and glory. God told Gideon that he still had too many men. I can imagine the initial shock that ten thousand Israeli soldiers was too many to fight the massive army of Midian, but God instructed Gideon to give his army another test. This time, the men were to get a drink of water from the river. Those who would cup their hand and bring the water to their mouth would stay, the remaining men that lapped water like a dog with their tongue could go home. After the test, Gideon was left with 300 men.

Gideon took the 300 men and drove the enemy away because the battle was the LORD's.

I remember a song from long ago that says,

"Little is much, when God is in it,
Labor not for wealth or fame.
There's a crown and you can win it,
When you go in Jesus' name."

Gideon, a *nobody* from nowhere, knew that the secret of success and victory is simply to do as the LORD commands.

Additional Scriptures

"Trust in the LORD with all thine heart; and lean not unto thine own understanding."
Proverbs 3:5

"Delight thyself also in the LORD; and he shall give thee the desires of thine heart. 5 Commit thy way unto the LORD; trust also in him; and he shall bring it to pass.
6 And he shall bring forth thy righteousness as the light, and thy judgment as the noonday."

Psalm 37:4-6

"The LORD is my strength and my shield; my heart trusted in him, and I am helped: therefore my heart greatly rejoiceth; and with my song will I praise him."
Psalm 28:7

"Charge them that are rich in this world, that they be not high-minded, nor trust in uncertain riches, but in the living God, who giveth us richly all things to enjoy;"
I Timothy 6:17

"What time I am afraid, I will trust in thee.
4 In God I will praise his word, in God I have put my trust; I will not fear what flesh can do unto me."
Psalm 56:3-4

"As for God, his way is perfect: the word of the LORD is tried: he is a buckler to all those that trust in him."
Psalm 18:30

Notes:

48

The Relevance of Antiquity

There is nothing quite like something that is very old. Some people collect old cars, trucks, and tractors. Others collect old dolls, old books, and antique furniture. There is just something special about these things that have been made long ago.

Another thing of antiquity is the Constitution of the United States. It was written as a guide for a new country to bring hope and prosperity to all its citizens.

The Bible is certainly from antiquity, and is quite relevant today. There is something else from antiquity that is relevant to our lives, but largely ignored today, and that is *Wisdom*.

The Book of Proverbs in the Bible is a wealth of knowledge worth finding out. The book encourages us to learn Wisdom. The first several chapters are devoted to the acquisition of Wisdom. Wisdom has a rich history, and that is where we begin. Proverbs 1:7,

> *"The fear of the LORD is the beginning of knowledge:*
> *but fools despise wisdom and instruction."*

Whether young or old, a fool is a fool. And a fool that cares not to learn of Wisdom is preparing a way for himself of despair and sorrow.

Wisdom is yearning to find her way to you. She is always there, patient, ever ready to be a part of you. But for those who do not care to embrace Wisdom, she said she would laugh at your calamity. However Wisdom also said this,

"But whoso hearkeneth (or listens and learns) *unto me shall dwell safely, and shall be quiet from fear of evil."*
Proverbs 1:33

This is a great promise from God, that Wisdom would allow you to dwell safely and lead a quiet and peaceful life. Further, Wisdom did not promise that you would be rich.

"Better is a dry morsel, and quietness therewith, than an house full of sacrifices with strife."
Proverbs 17:1

There are many people in this world whose lives are filled to the brim with strife. I am around people all the time with all kinds of difficulty; most self-induced.

Wisdom has been around for a long time. How Long?

"19 The LORD by wisdom hath founded the earth; by understanding hath he established the heavens. 20 By his knowledge the depths are broken up, and the clouds drop down the dew. 21 My son, let not

them depart from thine eyes: keep sound wisdom
and discretion:"
Proverbs 3:19-21

Wisdom gives knowledge and discretion. Discretion means, *"The freedom to decide what should be done in a particular situation."* There's nothing like a sound decision; the ability to think for yourself by godly principles, and then doing those things that are right unto the LORD.

"Trust in the LORD with all thine heart; and lean not
unto thine own understanding. In all thy ways
acknowledge him, and he shall direct thy paths."
Proverbs 3:5-6

My best counsel is that we cannot make the right decision without the Wisdom of the LORD. Search for it, seek it, find it, and hold on to it.
I like these verses in Proverbs that sum it up.

"5 Get wisdom, get understanding: forget it not;
neither decline from the words of my mouth. 6
Forsake her not, and she shall preserve thee: love
her, and she shall keep thee. 7 Wisdom is the
principal thing; therefore get wisdom: and with all
thy getting get understanding."
Proverbs 4:5-7

Relevant and sound words from Antiquity.

Additional Scriptures

"For the LORD giveth wisdom: out of his mouth cometh knowledge and understanding."
Proverbs 2:6

"If any of you lack wisdom, let him ask of God, that giveth to all men liberally."
James 1:5

"But the wisdom that is from above is first pure, then peaceable, gentle, and easy to be intreated, full of mercy and good fruits, without partiality, and without hypocrisy."
James 3:17

"How much better is it to get wisdom than gold! and to get understanding rather to be chosen than silver!"
Proverbs 16:16

"Walk in wisdom toward them that are without, redeeming the time. 6 Let your speech be alway with grace, seasoned with salt, that ye may know how ye ought to answer every man."
Colossians 4:5-6

"He that getteth wisdom loveth his own soul: he that keepeth understanding shall find good."
Proverbs 19:8

Notes:

49

Who Was The Wife of Cain?

I saw a preview for a television program this weekend where a rather smart mouthed girl was trying to prove a point by asking, "If Adam and Eve were the only people on earth, then who was the wife of Cain?" Actually, it's a good question. However, the question was asked in a *wise guy* sort of attitude.

There is a field of study called Apologetics, in which scholars will research the Bible for this and other answers. Christian people need this information so that they can give an answer when called to do so. There are many things not explained in the Scriptures that we must accept by faith. However, we are allowed to extrapolate many answers which are consistent with Bible Theology.

As for Cain, he is known for killing his brother Able because God did not accept Cain's offering. Cain became very angry and killed his brother. Even though we are not given God's early instructions for offerings, we know that when Adam and Eve sinned in the Garden of Eden, God made them coats of animal skins. Blood of the animal was shed in order to make the coats. The sacrifice of Able was accepted by God because it was of the fat of the flock. Cain's offering was the fruit of the ground.

A little later Cain left home and started a life of his own. As for his wife, he married his sister.

Today that practice would be frowned upon for it is against the law. There are good genetic reasons for that.

The Bible records the birth of males for the most part. There are a few instances where the Bible records the birth of females, but not often.

As for the first people on Earth, God created Adam and Eve on the sixth day of Creation. God instructed them to be fruitful and multiply, and they did just that. The Bible does not record all the names of male and female children that were born of Adam and Eve, but they were there. In fact, it is often forgotten that there was one born to take the place of Able, and his name is Seth. In Genesis Chapter 5 and verses 3 and 4,

"And Adam lived an hundred and thirty years, and begat a son in his own likeness, and after his image; and called his name Seth: 4 And the days of Adam after he had begotten Seth were eight hundred years: and he begat sons and daughters:"

We do not know how many children Adam and Eve produced, but with a lifespan of over 900 years, they no doubt had children in the hundreds.

We cannot take the *standards* of today and apply them to the ancients in the Bible. Cain's sister, which he took to wife, was of the first generation of humans. Adam and Eve's DNA was created pure and perfect by God. So there is no genetic problems with Cain and his sister being husband and wife.

There are other instances of close relatives being married. For example, the patriarch Abraham married his half-sister. In Genesis chapter 20 and verse 12 Abraham explains this to King Abimelech.

"And yet indeed she is my sister; she is the daughter of my father, but not the daughter of my mother; and she became my wife."

So Abraham and Sarai had the same father, but different mothers.

There are other close family marriages...Isaac married one of his distant cousins, Rebekah, as did Jacob marry distant cousins, Rachel and Leah. The DNA of all these people was still close to the Creation and remained reasonably pure. It wasn't until God gave the Law to Moses hundreds of years later that is was forbidden for someone to marry a relative. This law is in the book of Leviticus chapter 18 and verses 6-18. The passage is lengthy with many details. I think you can figure it out.

Finally, we need to study so that information such as this is on the tip of our tongue. When we appear afraid of the answer, the wolves will pounce.

Additional Scriptures

"So God created man in his own image, in the image of God created he him; male and female created he them. 28 And God blessed them, and God said unto them, Be fruitful, and multiply, and

replenish the earth, and subdue it: and have dominion over the fish of the sea, and over the fowl of the air, and over every living thing that moveth upon the earth."
Genesis 1:27-28

"What therefore God hath joined together, let not man put asunder."
Mark 10:9

"And above all things have fervent charity among yourselves: for charity shall cover the multitude of sins."
I Peter 4:8

"With all lowliness and meekness, with longsuffering, forbearing one another in love; 3 Endeavoring to keep the unity of the Spirit in the bond of peace."
Ephesians 4:2-3

"And if one prevail against him, two shall withstand him; and a threefold cord is not quickly broken."
Ecclesiastes 4:12

"Marriage is honourable in all, and the bed undefiled: but whoremongers and adulterers God will judge."
Hebrews 13:4

Notes:

50

Thousands or Millions?

I have an old timeline chart that shows the creation of the earth and the history of man up to the year 1900. I can see events in the Bible on the chart with the date of the event. The key to the chart is the genealogies in the Bible going all the way back to Adam. From the time of Adam until today, it is about 6000 years on the chart.

Today I heard a noted scientist say that the universe is 13.7 billion years old. Scientists have many reasons for coming up with that number. I believe that in time that number will rise to exceed 14 billion years or more. The number changes from time to time.

The question is: How old is the universe, and what difference does it make? Is it thousands of years, or millions and billions of years?

Science has made remarkable progress over the years. The fields of physics, astronomy, and more have made fascinating finds. I believe the mistake they have made is denying the existence of God. They would say that my mistake is believing in a Holy God. So which is right, and which is wrong?

The key to this struggle between religion and science is that believers in God believe by *faith*. We believe what God has given to us in His word, that it is true, accurate, and reliable. Anytime there is a debate between a scientist and a believer, it will always appear that the believer lost the debate because of his faith. The Bible is not accepted as the same authority for a non-believer.

I am secure in my faith, and a scientist can make it appear that I am a fool for doing so, but that is OK with me. It is not me they do not believe, it is The LORD God.

The Bible says,

"The fool hath said in his heart, There is no God."
Psalm 53:1a

I am sure this text would be very insulting to an atheistic scientist, but that *is* the Word of God.

Another question that surfaces is, what is the purpose of man? The purpose of man is to worship and be in fellowship with God. There is much comfort in the fact that God is not only Creator, but Redeemer of man. The only knowledge I need of the universe is that God created it just as He said. God created all things, and His words are completely true and accurate. God was there, so He is the faithful witness of creation. The account we have in the scripture is a firsthand witness of the six days of creation, and since His words are true and God does not lie, the account is completely reliable.

The witness we have of God within our being is something that the unbelieving scientist or any other unbeliever cannot understand. He has never experienced the joy that emanates from the Father, and spiritual union with the Creator of all things.

I don't fret at all when I hear scientist speak of their discoveries. They are not a threat to my faith. I do not understand *how* God brought all things into being. I know that He brought all things to be from nothingness. I know that He created all things for His glory. I know that when I gaze into the night sky I am thrilled at the handiwork of God. The stars, the moon, the occasional shooting star, all were created by Him and for Him.

God is in control of all things. He created them after all. Did God create the dinosaurs? Yes, on the sixth day of Creation. Did dinosaurs co-exist with man? Yes, beginning on the sixth day of creation. What made the dinosaurs go extinct? Most all dinosaurs were killed in Noah's flood, and the few that were on the Ark eventually died in the process of time after the flood.

I give honor, and glory, and praise to the Creator God. Amen.

Additional Scriptures

"The heavens declare the glory of God; and the firmament sheweth his handywork."
Psalm 19:1

"All things were made by him; and without him was not any thing made that was made."
John 1:3

"In the beginning God created the heaven and the earth."
Genesis 1:1

"By the word of the LORD were the heavens made; and all the host of them by the breath of his mouth."
Psalm 33:6

"Through faith we understand that the worlds were framed by the word of God, so that things which are seen were not made of things which do appear."
Hebrews 11:3

"Giving thanks unto the Father, which hath made us meet to be partakers of the inheritance of the saints in light: 13 Who hath delivered us from the power of darkness, and hath translated us into the kingdom of his dear Son: 14 In whom we have redemption through his blood, even the forgiveness of sins: 15 Who is the image of the invisible God, the firstborn of every creature: 16 For by him were all things created, that are in heaven, and that are in earth, visible and invisible, whether they be thrones, or dominions, or principalities, or powers: all things were created by him, and for him: 17 And he is before all things, and by him all things consist."
Colossians 1:12-17

Notes:

51

Of Dirt and Bone

My mom served as a pastor's wife for 42 years and, since Dad's retirement, has assisted him over the last 10 years with his ministry of preaching at various churches. She has also conducted numerous ladies conferences, published a couple of books, and taught numerous people how to play the piano. Through all this she has acquired much theological wisdom. So, here we are talking of dirt and bone.

Mom noticed many years ago while doing the laundry that Dad would get *ring around the collar* on his white shirts while she did not get *ring around the collar* on her white blouses and other garments. She remembered reading in Genesis Chapter 2 about the creation of man and woman and came up with a breakthrough explanation about the *ring around the collar* phenomenon.

The Bible says in Genesis Chapter 2 verse 7,

"And the LORD God formed man of the dust of the ground, and breathed into his nostrils the breath of life; and man became a living soul."

So the Bible is clear; man is made out of dust and dirt. That explains the *ring around the collar* because every time a man wears a shirt some of the dirt rubs off!

But wait! What is the explanation for the woman NOT having *ring around the collar*? Mom read further in Genesis chapter 2 verses 21 and 22, "And the LORD God caused a deep sleep to fall upon Adam, and he slept: and he took one of his ribs, and closed up the flesh instead thereof; 22 And the rib, which the LORD God had taken from man, made he a woman, and brought her unto the man."

There it is: woman is made from bone and bone does not rub off. That's why women don't get *ring around the collar*!

There is something else you need to know beyond this whimsical analysis. God also said that the man would leave his mother and father and cleave, or hold tightly, to his wife. God also said they would be one flesh. God made the woman a very special creation. The man should hold his wife close to his side, from whence came the rib, and care for her, love her, honor her, and treat her with all kindness and gentleness. The man should see that her needs are met and provide the security she desires. The woman should also do those things that honor her husband. Proverbs chapter 31 verses 10 thru 31 speaks of the virtuous woman whose value is far above rubies. It is worth reading, I promise.

No doubt men and women are different in many ways, but God created man and woman to complement and complete each other.

Ladies, I hope you take pride in your man as you use the stain remover on the collar of his shirts.

It's a sign that sometime somewhere he worked up a sweat and some of him rubbed off!

And guys, a heads up that Valentine's Day is always on February 14. Be sure to honor your mate with a card and flowers, and let her know how much you truly appreciate her being a part of your life.

Additional Scriptures

"Submitting yourselves one to another in the fear of God. 22 Wives, submit yourselves unto your own husbands, as unto the Lord.23 For the husband is the head of the wife, even as Christ is the head of the church: and he is the saviour of the body. 24 Therefore as the church is subject unto Christ, so let the wives be to their own husbands in every thing. 25 Husbands, love your wives, even as Christ also loved the church, and gave himself for it; 26 That he might sanctify and cleanse it with the washing of water by the word, 27 That he might present it to himself a glorious church, not having spot, or wrinkle, or any such thing; but that it should be holy and without blemish."
Ephesians 5:21-27

"Therefore shall a man leave his father and his mother, and shall cleave unto his wife: and they shall be one flesh. 25 And they were both naked, the man and his wife, and were not ashamed."
Genesis 2:24-25

"For the man is not of the woman; but the woman of the man."
I Corinthians 11:8

"But now, O LORD, thou art our father; we are the clay, and thou our potter; and we all are the work of thy hand."
Isaiah 64:8

"Thine hands have made me and fashioned me together round about; yet thou dost destroy me. 9 Remember, I beseech thee, that thou hast made me as the clay; and wilt thou bring me into dust again?"
Job 10:8-9

"Thy hands have made me and fashioned me: give me understanding, that I may learn thy commandments."
Psalm 119:73

Notes:

52

A Christmas Blessing

When Jesus was born in Bethlehem around two thousand years ago, God fulfilled a promise and bestowed a blessing upon all the inhabitants of the earth. The promise and the blessing were both accomplished in Jesus.

The Bible gives us in Isaiah and Luke these promises that would be fulfilled with the birth of Jesus Christ.

"For unto us a child is born, unto us a son is given: and the government shall be upon his shoulder: and his name shall be called Wonderful, Counsellor, The mighty God, The everlasting Father, The Prince of Peace."
Isaiah 9:6

Glory to God in the highest, and on Earth peace, good will toward men."
Luke 2:14

This promise of peace and goodness is the blessing that is given to all mankind; and yes, it is given to you.

Christmas is a wonderful time of year, but sometimes we become encumbered with the trappings of the season rather than the peace and goodness that is given to us through Jesus Christ.

There are many pressures and distractions directed toward us that we must process in our minds during this season. The pressures of merchandisers is enormous: longer store hours, sales, long lines, endless advertising, and instant credit. Many people will spend money they don't have, to buy things that people don't need, to make impressions that don't matter, and end up with bills in January as the reward for it all.

As the events of this world seem to be moving at an ever faster pace, perhaps you might try what God has offered to you.

"Be still, and know that I am God."
Psalm 46:10

I encourage you to do just that. Slow down, be still, and discover who God is. He desires the best for us including His Goodness and Peace.

I have a tradition I practice at First Baptist, Roxton and that is to ask God to bless the people after Sunday services. I would now desire that God would bless you and your home this Christmas Holiday. I pray that God will bless you and keep you, that God would make His face to shine upon you and be gracious to you, and that God would give you peace in your life and in your home. Amen.

Additional Scriptures

"For the grace of God that bringeth salvation hath appeared to all men, 12 Teaching us that, denying ungodliness and worldly lusts, we should live soberly, righteously, and godly, in this present world; 13 Looking for that blessed hope, and the glorious appearing of the great God and our Saviour Jesus Christ;"
Titus 2:11-13

"Blessed be the God and Father of our Lord Jesus Christ, who hath blessed us with all spiritual blessings in heavenly places in Christ:"
Ephesians 1:3

"The grace of the Lord Jesus Christ, and the love of God, and the communion of the Holy Ghost, be with you all. Amen."
II Corinthians 13:14

"For the law was given by Moses, but grace and truth came by Jesus Christ."
John 1:17

"Honour the LORD with thy substance, and with the firstfruits of all thine increase: 10 So shall thy barns be filled with plenty, and thy presses shall burst out with new wine."
Proverbs 3:9-10

"Beloved, I wish above all things that thou mayest prosper and be in health, even as thy soul prospereth."
III John verse 2

Notes:

ABOUT THE AUTHOR

Louis A. Holmes was born in 1954 in a hot and dry West Texas town where his dad worked in the oil fields. His formative years were spent as a preacher's kid in the small North Texas town of Grapevine. Presently, he is the bi-vocational Pastor of First Baptist Church in Roxton, Texas. Raised in a preacher's home, he has many life experiences to draw from, all with an application to God's Word.

Jan, his wife of 41 years, has been an important part of his ministry. They have three children, Eric, Erin, and Michelle. Louis and Jan also have two grandchildren, Jovie and Zed.

The Church in Roxton asked Bro. Louis, as he likes to be called, to write and publish an encouraging article in the Roxton newspaper, The Roxton Progress. God has truly blessed the effort, and Bro. Louis is praying that the articles are making a difference in the lives of his readers.

www.ingramcontent.com/pod-product-compliance
Lightning Source LLC
Chambersburg PA
CBHW031953040426
42448CB00006B/339